"And Then Seve Told Freddie..."

A Collection of the Greatest True Golf Stories Ever Told

DON WADE

Foreword by Peter Jacobsen

D1113609

CONTEMPORARY BOOKS

Library of Congress Cataloging-in-Publication Data

Wade, Don.
    And then Seve told Freddie— : a collection of the greatest true
golf stories ever told / Don Wade ; foreword by Peter Jacobsen.
      p.   cm.
    Includes index.
    ISBN 0-8092-3147-6 (cloth)
    ISBN 0-8092-2871-8 (paper)
    1. Golf—Anecdotes.   2. Golfers—Anecdotes.   I. Title.
GV967.W267   1997
796.352—dc21   97-17533
                                               CIP

Front cover photo by Steve Szurlej
Author photo by Dom Furore
Illustrations by Paul Szep

Published by Contemporary Books
A division of NTC/Contemporary Publishing Group, Inc.
4255 West Touhy Avenue, Lincolnwood (Chicago), Illinois 60646-1975 U.S.A.
Copyright © 1998 by Don Wade
Printed in the United States of America
International Standard Book Number: 0-8092-3147-6 (cloth)
                                       0-8092-2871-8 (paper)

18   17   16   15   14   13   12   11   10   9   8   7   6   5   4   3   2   1

This one's for all the Golf Guys.

CONTENTS

FOREWORD

Everyone has their dream pairing—the three people they'd absolutely love to play a round of golf with. For most people, I suspect, it would be three players from their personal Top Ten list.

That's fine, but if I had my way I just might pick Sam Snead, Jimmy Demaret, and, let's say, Lee Trevino. Nothing against all the other great players, but can you imagine the stories you'd hear from these guys? You'd be falling down laughing so often that you'd need six hours just to get the round in—with plenty of stories left over for the locker room. How perfect would that day be?

That's one reason I'm so happy to write this Foreword for *"And Then Seve Told Freddie . . ."*, the fifth book in Don Wade's wonderful collections of golf anecdotes. Aside from being fun to read, I think these books really give readers a feel for the game of golf—the highs and lows; the funny side and the sad side, too.

I hope you enjoy this book, and that you take away a few stories to share with your friends the next time you play—it will make the round more fun for everyone.

—Peter Jacobsen

PREFACE

Anyone who has paid even the slightest attention to the game of golf knows that it is experiencing a remarkable period of growth. Kids are taking up the game. So are women. And so are guys of the baby-boom generation whose bodies and egos have finally taken enough beatings on the playing fields of middle age. A word of advice to all of them: golf only appears easy—and therein lies a large part of the fascination with the game.

There are a lot of very good reasons to take up golf—at any age. But the worst possible reason is one that keeps popping up with a depressing regularity.

"I took up the game because it will help my career."

Well, no, it won't. Not unless your career happens to be playing golf for a living, and there's not many of us lucky enough to do that. The bizarre notion that you can make the Deal of the Century on the golf course is a tired cliché. It is the stuff of a *New Yorker* cartoon . . . and an old *New Yorker* cartoon, at that.

If you are taking up golf as some sort of Dale Carnegie course, you are badly missing the point. You should take up golf because it's a great way to be with friends. Or meet new friends. Or be alone when you need to be alone.

It's a magical way to spend time with your kids when

they're young and they need to spend time with you. And it's a special way to spend time with them when you're older, and finally realize just how little time you have been given with them in a world where the demands are all so great.

You can play the game with your wife or husband.

You cannot, however, give them lessons. There's a limit to love.

You should take up the game because you can follow it to beautiful places: Places where the sunlight sparks across the water and the shadows fall deep and long in the early evening. Places where the new green leaves welcome spring. Places where the fall colors brilliantly mark the end of another season. Places that are serene, especially when blanketed in the deepest snows of winter.

You should take up the game because it helps you understand and appreciate the great champions and championships. People like Jones, Hagen, Sarazen, and Ouimet; Snead, Nelson, and Hogan; Palmer, Nicklaus, Watson, Trevino, and so many more. Players who tested themselves and triumphed at special places like St. Andrews and Muirfield; Augusta, Brookline, Merion, Winged Foot, and Pebble Beach.

And you should take up the game because, most of all, it's honest: just you, a club, a ball, a hole, and a scorecard. Nothing else in life is that simple. Or that complicated.

I hope you enjoy the book. And I hope these stories help make the game a little more special for you.

ACKNOWLEDGMENTS

This is the fifth book in a series that began in 1991 with the publication of *"And Then Jack Said to Arnie . . ."*, and over the years there have been some remarkable constants.

Nancy Crossman, my editor at Contemporary Books, bet on the first book and has been the series' biggest fan. More important, she's been a great friend. Every writer deserves an editor like Nancy Crossman. Everyone deserves a friend like Nancy Crossman.

Paul Szep's drawings have graced these books, just as they have enlivened the editorial page of the *Boston Globe* since 1968. That's almost thirty years of bringing misery to the rich and famous and a measure of revenge to the rest of us. Paul grew up in Canada, so, naturally, when he was invited to a reception at the Reagan White House, his parents were very proud of their son. His mother told a neighbor that Paul was going to Washington.

"Oh, does he work for the government now?" the neighbor asked Mrs. Szep.

"Heavens no," said Mrs. Szep. "He's a cartoonist. He works against the government."

It's great to be a fan of Szep. It's better to be a friend of Szep.

If anyone ever sat down and wrote the job description for

being an agent, there would be no agents, and writers wouldn't be taken care of by people like Chris Tomasino. She's a protector and cheerleader; an editor and critic; a dear and loyal friend.

During the past fifteen or so years that Steve Szurlej has been a photographer with *Golf Digest*, he's probably taken every type of golf photograph imaginable. He's captured the great moments at the Major championships. He's shot swing sequences of the game's champions and stunningly beautiful photos of the game's classic courses. Happily, he also shot the covers for this series of books. Those covers, more than anything else, capture the sense of friendship and camaraderie that is at the core of the game.

Peter Jacobsen is a formidable storyteller in his own right, so it only made sense to have him write the Foreword. He joins Lee Trevino, Gary McCord, Ken Venturi, and Curtis Strange, who were also good enough to help out on these books. Thanks again to all of you.

And thanks to all the Golf Guys—the people who are lucky enough to make a living around golf—for all the help over all the years.

Finally, thanks to Julia, Ben, Darcy, and Andy, and also all the Concord Wades, for their love, support, patience, and understanding.

AMY ALCOTT

A my Alcott is one of the great characters in women's
golf—or in all of golf, for that matter. Not the least of
her attributes is a wicked sense of humor and a great sense
of comic timing.

One day she called a writer friend to tell him that she'd
just been named the top female Jewish athlete in the United
States.

"Congratulations, Amy," the friend said. "That's great.
Who'd you beat?"

"Some fencer from Brandeis," she deadpanned.

ARCHITECTS

Celebrated golf course architect Robert Trent Jones has received a number of challenging assignments over his long career, but it's doubtful any have been as severe a test as a course he was asked to build in Sardinia for the Aga Khan.

The site was mountainous, with steep rocky hillsides. Previous architects had said that the only way to build a course on the site was to import hundreds of tons of soil. Trent Jones had a better idea. He ordered that the tops of the mountains be dynamited and the resulting rocks be pulverized with a rock-crushing machine. It was a masterstroke, both of imagination and of design, and it resulted in a fine course that saved the Aga Khan hundreds of thousands of dollars.

One time Jones was in a hospital for a routine physical when he got a call from a friend who wanted Jones to meet him to discuss a potentially lucrative assignment. Jones, ignoring his doctor's orders, threw on a topcoat over his hospital gown and took off for the meeting.

In the early 1940s, Robert Trent Jones designed a course for a growing young company called IBM, near their headquarters in Poughkeepsie, New York. Jones worked closely with the company's president, Thomas Watson.

At one point, Jones and Watson were walking the property and Watson pointed to a fairly large hill and suggested that it be used as a site for one of the tees. Jones politely suggested that it might be just a little too much of a hike to get to the tee.

"Nonsense," said Watson. "The whole point of this game is to get exercise, isn't it?"

Jones, ever the diplomat, suggested they climb the hill for a better look. Several minutes later, when the exhausted group reached the top of the hill, Watson admitted that Jones was right and told him to route the course any way he wanted.

When the project was completed, Jones presented a bill for his fee—$13,000. Watson offered to pay him in IBM stock, but Jones decided to take the cash.

Years later, it would prove to be a costly decision, as IBM stock became some of the most valuable in American history.

Canadian architect Stanley Baldwin had a great sense of humor—which was occasionally lost on some of his benefactors. Baldwin designed a number of courses for the Canadian National Railway, and the directors were generally quite happy with his work. One exception was Jasper Park, where he designed the 9th hole so it would resemble the figure of a particularly famous actress. The head of the railway demanded that the hole be modified, but to this day it's still known as "Cleopatra."

Over the years, architect Robert Trent Jones has occasionally been confused with Robert Tyre Jones. This was especially true when the two men collaborated on Peachtree Golf Club in Atlanta in 1945.

The two men met in the clubhouse at Bobby Jones's home course, East Lake, and then headed onto the course. After making the turn, a group of members appeared just as the architect hit his tee shot close to the hole on a par 3.

"Fellows, this is Bob Jones, the architect," Bobby Jones said.

At that moment it occurred to both men that they had to find a way to alleviate the confusion.

"Bob, there can only be one Bobby Jones in Atlanta, and that's you," the architect said. "From now on, just call me Trent. It's an old family name."

Robert Trent Jones has designed courses all over the world, and over the years has rubbed elbows with some of the world's most powerful leaders—although not always without incident.

In the early 1970s, he designed forty-five holes at Royal Golf Dar Es Salaam in Rabat for King Hassan II of Morocco. Jones soon struck up a friendship with the King, who invited him to one of his palaces for a birthday party.

When he reached the palace, he tried to enter the grounds in his rental car, but was turned away by guards and directed to a public lot. When he reached the course where a tournament was being played, he was confronted by a group of soldiers, who soon began firing in the direction of the palace.

Jones assumed it was part of the festivities, until the troops ordered him and some other guests to a remote part of the property at gunpoint. In the background they could hear gunfire and grenade explosions.

A soldier approached Jones and demanded his passport.

"Diplomat?" he asked after studying the document.

"Yes, American diplomat," Jones said, trying to maintain his composure.

With that he was led away from the others. An hour or so later, a second group of soldiers came along, shouting, "The King is alive! God save the King!"

It was only then that Jones learned that he had been caught up in the middle of an attempted coup.

The education of golf course architects comes in a fascinating variety of fashions. This was particularly true until recent years; today, more and more architects are learning their craft in college.

To be sure, Dr. Alister Mackenzie's education was unusual by any standard. Mackenzie, a Scotsman, was serving with British forces in South Africa during the Boer War of the late nineteenth century. He became fascinated by the Boers' use of camouflage to hide their defensive emplacements from British artillery.

"I came to understand the remarkable resemblance between the use of military camouflage and the design of a good golf hole," he once observed.

Following the war, Mackenzie put his knowledge to work in his designs for some of the world's greatest courses— courses like Augusta National, Royal Melbourne, and Cypress Point.

It's been said that every great artist is at least a little eccentric. Maybe it's because they see the world from a slightly different slant or perspective. Whatever the reason, it can fairly be said that architect A. W. Tillinghast was eccentric—to say the least.

The man who designed such masterpieces as the two courses at Winged Foot and its neighbor, Quaker Ridge, was born to wealth and then managed to accumulate a fortune of his own. As befits a man of his stature, he both dressed and acted the part.

He invariably dressed in expensive, three-piece suits and was driven to his New York City office by chauffeured limousine. If his plans called for him to visit a course site that day, it didn't alter his choice of clothes. He'd motor out to the construction site, march imperiously into the woods and fields, find a shady spot, and begin shouting orders to the laborers—interrupting his instructions just long enough to sip whiskey from a silver flask he always carried with him.

Eccentric? Sure. But in what was surely the golden age of American golf-course architecture, Tillinghast's designs were unsurpassed.

AUGUSTA NATIONAL GOLF CLUB

Even from the first days of Augusta National Golf Club's existence, when Bob Jones and Clifford Roberts were calling the shots, the people who run the club have set very high standards for every aspect of the club's operation—as writer Ken Bowden once found out.

Bowden, a transplanted Brit who came to America to work for *Golf Digest*, collaborated with Clifford Roberts on the club's official history, *The History of Augusta National*. Bowden thought the manuscript was complete until he received a phone call from Roberts summoning him to Augusta from his home in Connecticut. Bowden was baffled. He reviewed his copy of the manuscript and was confident it was what Roberts and the publisher had asked him to produce. Nevertheless, he made the trip south. When he arrived at the club, he promptly met with Roberts and discovered just what it was that Roberts wanted changed.

Six punctuation marks.

The friendship between Bob Jones and Clifford Roberts dated back to Jones's playing days. Roberts was keenly aware of Jones's often-expressed desire to someday help design and build a course capable of hosting a championship. Finally, after much searching, they came across some property on the site of an old nursery in Augusta.

"Why don't you build your course down here?" Roberts asked. "It's not far from Atlanta, and you'll be able to get over here as often as you like."

"I'll build it if you'll finance it," said Jones.

"That will teach me to make a careless remark," Roberts replied.

Clifford Roberts was a demanding taskmaster, and he wasn't exactly known as a funny guy. Still, he had an interesting sense of humor, which often came through at the club's annual Jamboree. One year he arranged for a movie crew to film players driving off a tee set back into the trees. As each group arrived on the tee, a man in a bear suit charged out from the azaleas, startling the players.

The man in the bear suit was Clifford Roberts.

One year during the Masters, Clifford Roberts heard reports that some people in the gallery were making a lot of noise and bothering the players. Roberts drove out to investigate; when he got there, he discovered that the culprits were comedian and television star Jackie Gleason and some of his friends. Roberts took their badges and ordered the Pinkerton guards to escort them off the property.

"This is the Augusta National, not Broadway," he told Gleason.

Augusta National and CBS operate under a series of one-year contracts. This gives the club enormous leverage when it comes to making suggestions on how the telecasts might be improved.

One year it occurred to Roberts that someone of unusual stature was needed to open the telecast. But whoever he had in mind was a far cry from the person CBS proposed: Ed Sullivan, whose variety show was one of the longest-running hits on the CBS schedule.

"Ed Sullivan?" Roberts replied. "Never. Why, the man has monkey acts on his show."

One of the charming Masters traditions is that every champion is invited to play in the tournament, regardless of age. As of 1996, Sam Snead and Doug Ford have both played in forty-four tournaments.

Having said that, tournament officials expect a player to know when the time has come to become a ceremonial participant and open a place in the field for a younger player. One player who was slow to take the hint was Ralph Guldahl, who won the 1939 Masters.

As the years went by, Guldahl continued to compete, oblivious to the urgings of Clifford Roberts. Finally, Roberts had seen enough. He sent Guldahl out in the last pairing of the day, then ordered the enormous fairway mowers to follow him closely for his entire round.

Guldahl got the message. Loud and clear, as it were.

By almost everyone's reckoning, the Masters is the best-run tournament in the world—in part because it's the only Major championship played on the same course every year, but also because tournament officials have never hesitated to make changes and improvements. Take, for example, their decision to institute the "10 Shot Rule," which allows any player within ten shots of the leader to make the thirty-six-hole cut. Of course, the decision wasn't made for entirely altruistic reasons.

It stemmed from the year that amateur Don Cherry made a fifteen-foot birdie putt on the 18th hole, which eliminated—among other players—Ben Hogan and Dr. Cary Middlecoff, two of the biggest attractions in the field.

One of the biggest stories in the early days of the Masters was the Calcutta, where people would bet—often enormous sums—on their favorite players.

In 1946, Herman Keiser went to the big Calcutta party and saw that the odds on his winning were 20 to 1. A frugal man by nature, he sprang for a mere $20. He shot 68-69 in the first two rounds to take a five-shot lead over Ben Hogan, who was in second place.

The next morning, the two men running the Calcutta approached Keiser and told him there had been a huge amount of money bet on Hogan. One member alone had bet $40,000 on Hogan.

"They asked if there was anything they could do to help me out," Keiser remembers. "I thought about it for a minute and then asked them if I could get $50 down on me at the same 20-to-1 odds. I told them that if I couldn't hang on to a five-shot lead, I didn't deserve to win, Hogan or no Hogan. They let me make the bet."

He was paired with Byron Nelson in the final round, and hit the pin with his approach to the final hole. The ball stopped thirty feet from the cup.

"Herman, is it true that you haven't three-putted once this week?" Nelson asked as they walked toward the green.

"Yep, but I've still got some work left," Keiser said.

Naturally, he three-putted the hole.

"Poor Byron was beside himself," says Keiser. "He was sure he'd jinxed me and cost me the tournament. He must have apologized a dozen times."

Keiser was sitting with his friend Henry Picard in the clubhouse as Hogan played the 18th, tied with Keiser for the lead.

"Let's go watch and see how Ben does," said Picard.

"No, thanks, you go watch and let me know," said Keiser.

A few minutes later, Picard came back into the clubhouse.

"He made a heck of a putt, Herman—for a five."

Keiser won $1,500—and a healthy Calcutta payoff.

Just prior to the start of the 1974 Masters, a London bookmaker listed the odds of 1972 British Amateur champion Trevor Homer winning the Masters at 5,000 to 1.

Homer disagreed.

"Five million to one would be more bloody like it," said Homer.

But Homer did notice another bet that seemed more to his liking. The bookies were offering odds of 3 to 1 that, based on his performance the previous year (81-88-cut), he wouldn't break 80 in his first two rounds.

Homer shot rounds of 77 and 72. He missed the cut, but he emerged with his honor intact—and possibly a little richer for his efforts.

Herman Keiser's win came in the first Masters held following World War II. That's not to say that Augusta National and its most prominent member—Bob Jones— didn't play a part in the war effort.

Jones, at age forty, was well beyond draft age, but he volunteered and served as a lieutenant colonel in the Army Air Force, landing on Normandy Beach just twenty-four hours after the first wave of forces landed on D day.

As for Augusta National, the course was closed for play and for three years was used as grazing land for cattle.

Over the years, a number of changes have been made to the Augusta National course. The nines were flip-flopped shortly after the course opened. Architect Robert Trent Jones was brought in to change the par-3 16th hole in 1947. He moved the tee to the left, lengthening the hole, and expanded a creek into a beautiful—and dangerous—pond. Of course, this change didn't occur without some complications.

"While we were excavating the pond, an enormous series of thunderstorms moved through the area," Trent Jones recalled. "The rains came so fast and so hard that we didn't have time to move a tractor we had been using. Before too long, the tractor was totally underwater. It took a few days before we could pull it out."

The original design for Augusta National that Bobby Jones and Dr. Alister Mackenzie developed included a 19th hole—a short par 3 to be used if a match was tied after eighteen holes. Such holes were not uncommon at the time Augusta National was built. For some reason, the hole was never built at Augusta. The bets somehow manage to get settled anyway.

One year at the Champions' Dinner, a player was discussing the short but difficult par-4 3rd hole with Bob Jones. He said the hole bothered him because he felt he should come

off of it with a birdie, and yet he was always reliev
a par.

"But you're not supposed to make a 3 there," Jones said, grinning. "There are just some holes that are supposed to be par 3s, no matter how short they might be."

For many years, the menu at the Champions' Dinner was virtually unchanged. Strip steaks were always served, as were canned peaches.

"Cliff Roberts always claimed that we had peaches because they were Bob Jones's favorite dessert," said one past champion. "But the rumor was that Cliff got a great deal on peaches one year and had hundreds of cans of the damn things stored in the clubhouse."

The par-3 12th hole is one of the most infamous holes at Augusta National. Balls that come up short find a bunker—if a player is lucky—but more often than not they roll down the steep slope and into a pond. Behind the green is only slightly better—a bunker, trees, and shrubs await. To make matters even more complicated, the winds swirl around the green, making club selection difficult.

For most of its history, people have credited the hole's difficulty entirely to the design by Bobby Jones and Dr. Alister Mackenzie. Now it turns out that there's a spiritual reason as well: the green was built upon the site of an old Indian burial ground.

For many years, Augusta National was criticized because an African American had never been invited to compete in the Masters. Clifford Roberts defended the club, arguing that no African American had qualified for an invitation and that making an exception would amount to tokenism. Be that as it may, the issue served as an annual source of contention between the club and its critics.

It became a moot point, however, when Lee Elder won a tournament in 1974, making him eligible for an invitation to the 1975 Masters. Naturally, Elder's arrival for the Masters that April was the dominant pretournament story. Less known, however, was an unreported act of kindness by Roberts.

Knowing that Elder would be under considerable pressure and hoping desperately that he'd play well, Roberts contacted Elder and invited him to come to Augusta National months ahead of the tournament so he could familiarize himself with the course and the surroundings without the distractions of the press and the galleries.

Almost twenty years later, the club resolved another source of controversy by accepting its first African American member, Ron Townsend.

SEVE BALLESTEROS

When Seve Ballesteros tied for second at the 1976 British Open at Royal Birkdale, the nineteen-year-old Spaniard was instantly billed as the "Next Great Player." And while he was certainly talented and charismatic, the verdict remained out for more than a few writers—at least until he went head-to-head with a forty-seven-year-old Arnold Palmer at the Lancome Trophy tournament in Paris a short while after the British Open.

After falling 4-down, Ballesteros staged a magnificent comeback over the final nine holes. He birdied 12 and 13 and, after making another birdie on 15, the match was all square. After he birdied 17, he knew he had broken Palmer's spirit.

"I knew I had won the match when I saw him shake his head and look at the ground," said Ballesteros later. "That was when I knew I finally had him beaten."

For his part, Palmer was both gracious and prescient in his praise of Ballesteros—who would go on to win three British Opens and two Masters.

"I threw everything I could at him," said Palmer. "I hit every green on the back nine and he never flinched. Not once."

According to those who know him, Seve Ballesteros has burned to be a champion almost from the moment the youngster picked up an old 3-iron and began hitting golf balls along the beaches near his home. It was beyond ambition, even beyond the considerable ambitions that drive other champions to succeed. It was as though he had to prove something—to himself and to others. Maybe he wanted to prove that a Spanish golfer could beat the best the rest of the world could offer. Maybe it had its roots deeper than that, in Spain's fairly rigid caste system.

Whatever the reason, Seve was uncommonly driven and competitive. After his first big tournament, the Spanish PGA Championship, one of his brothers found him sobbing and disconsolate in the locker room.

He had lost.

He was 17.

PEGGY KIRK BELL

Peggy Kirk Bell is one of the great women of the game. After a fine amateur career, she was a successful player on the fledgling LPGA Tour—playing against the likes of Babe Zaharias, Louise Suggs, and Patty Berg. After leaving competitive golf, she and her late husband, Bullet, bought the venerable Pine Needles resort in Southern Pines, North Carolina, where they raised their family. Peggy Kirk Bell established herself as one of the game's best teachers as well as one of golf's most respected ambassadors. She has received the United States Golf Association's highest honor, the Bob Jones Award, and, in 1996, Pine Needles hosted the U.S. Women's Open.

"One of the most remarkable people I've met in golf was Glenna Collett Vare," Peggy Kirk Bell remembers. "In 1950, she was captain of the Curtis Cup team that played the team from Great Britain and Ireland at the Country Club of Buffalo in Williamsville, New York. I was a member of the team, and I was scared to death. I begged her not to play me in the singles matches, but she wouldn't hear of it. 'I'm the captain, and you're playing,' she told me.

"She came out to the 16th hole to see how I was doing, and I signaled to her that I was 1-down. I felt terrible. A couple of minutes later, she came up and gave me a four-leaf clover she'd found. I went on to win the match, 1-up. I still have that four-leaf clover, too."

TOMMY BOLT

Over the years, few players ever attracted as much attention for a bad temper as Tommy Bolt. Not only did he attract more than his share of fines from Tour officials, but he actually seemed to revel in the attention.

After one particularly costly run of fines, the Tour threatened to really crack down if there were any more displays of club throwing, so Bolt's friends decided to help out. Tommy was paired with Porky Oliver in a tournament, and he hit a poor shot. Oliver, sensing that Bolt was about to do some serious damage to his clubs, did the only logical thing. He walked over to where Bolt's bag lay on the ground and gently toed it into a shallow creek.

THE BOYS

I can't prove this, but I'm willing to bet that every club in America has a group of guys like "The Boys" at my club in Connecticut. The Boys are mainstays of the place. They rarely miss a round of golf on the weekend. They're rarely lacking for an opinion on how the place is being run. The club's restaurant/bar budget couldn't come close to balancing without them, and they provide whatever club they belong to—whether it's a Winged Foot, a Garden City, or wherever—with much of the club's character. You don't have to be single to be one of The Boys—although it helps. Failing that, an understanding wife will do. My friend, Dennis Powell, is one of The Boys.

At one time we had a locker-room attendant who, it's safe to say, didn't specialize in the care and upkeep of shoes. Given his job description, this was something of a problem.

One afternoon, Dennis arrived with three guests. Since he worked on Wall Street and these were important clients, he wasn't taking any chances.

"Hi," he said to the attendant as they entered the locker room. "Here's $20. Don't touch the shoes."

All this might seem excessive, unless you understand what he had been through when he visited another club for a tournament. I should note here that The Boys spend much of their time playing in tournaments all over the place. The host pros love them because they always spend lavishly on shirts, sweaters, bags, and all that stuff. It helps to have discretionary income if you're going to be one of The Boys.

"I showed up at this tournament with a shirt from Pine Valley, a belt from Merion, and a hat from Shinnecock," Dennis said. "When I was changing my shoes, the locker-room guy asked me how everything was at my club. I asked him how he knew what club I was from.

"'Your shoes,' he said."

If you're one of The Boys, there are few fates in the world worse than playing golf with a woman. In fact, there may be nothing in life—short of an IRS audit—that holds more terror. For them, just being around a club during a mixed tournament is a near-death experience.

One day Dennis and some friends were out on Long Island where they came across a place that offered bungee jumping. Now, even though it was late in the day and more than a few beers had gone by the wayside, even Dennis could see that bungee jumping wasn't a pastime designed for a middle-aged man. And no amount of cajoling or insulting was going to change his mind—until he received the ultimate threat.

"Dennis, you wussie, either go up there and jump or you've got to play golf with me this weekend," said a woman friend.

And that was Dennis Powell's introduction to bungee jumping.

JACK BURKE JR.

There's always been a certain irrefutable logic to the thinking of Jackie Burke, the winner of both the 1956 Masters and PGA Championship.

On the verge of the 1997 season, Steve Elkington, a friend and admirer, told Burke that his clubs had been stolen.

"So what?" Burke said. "You weren't winning with them anyway. Good riddance."

Sure enough, Elkington got a new set and won in Los Angeles and at The Players Championship.

JACK BURKE SR.

Jack Burke Sr. was one of the game's top teaching professionals, widely respected both in Texas and across the
country.

One day a man approached Burke and asked for a lesson.

"What system do you teach?" the man asked Burke.

"My only system is no system at all," Burke said. "Only lazy
people have systems."

CADDIES

For the first forty-eight years of the Masters, players were required to use caddies from the club instead of their regular Tour caddies. One of the best was Pappy Stokes, who was born and raised next to Augusta National. Pappy was a particular favorite of Clifford Roberts, and took his role as one of the senior caddies very seriously. If a caddie misbehaved, Pappy would shoot him a look—and a warning.

"Boy, God's got his eyes on you," he'd say.

One time a guest came to Augusta, and as he walked down the first fairway he asked his caddie what the other caddie's name was.

"Cemetery," he replied.

"How'd he get that name?" the guest asked.

"One night he was with a woman and her husband came around and slit his throat," the caddie explained. "We thought he was dead, so when he got out of the hospital we started calling him Cemetery."

"Is that true?" the guest asked Cemetery.

"No, sir," Cemetery protested. "It wasn't his wife."

Several years ago, there was a player on the Tour who had a reputation for throwing clubs. As a result, he had a hard time getting and keeping caddies at the Masters. Finally, he hooked up with a young caddie who stuck with him. One of his fellow caddies asked him why.

"Because he pays as good as he throws," said the caddie.

In 1961, Gary Player came to the par-3 16th hole at Augusta National in contention to win his first Masters. As he looked over his par putt on Sunday, he told his caddie he thought he should play it on the left edge.

"No, Mr. Player," the caddie replied. "It's right edge all the way."

Player disagreed.

"Trust me, Mr. Player," the caddie insisted. "It's right edge. If you put it there and it doesn't go in, I'm working for free this week—and you know I can't afford that."

Player started the ball at the right edge and it dropped into the cup.

"It was the most important putt I made all week," Player said later.

When Ben Hogan arrived at Carnoustie for the 1953 British Open, he drew a caddie by the name of Cecil Timms. While they were a successful team, it wasn't exactly a marriage made in heaven.

Hogan seldom spoke on the course. Timms never shut up.

Hogan put tins of hard candy in his bag to keep his energy up. Timms ate most of the candies.

Worst of all, when Hogan settled over a putt, Timms would cover his eyes.

Finally, it got to be too much for Hogan.

"Cecil, I want you to do three things for me," he said. "Stand still, keep your eyes open, and keep your mouth shut."

In the 1971 Masters, Charlie Coody had a caddie named Cricket Pritchett, an Atlanta bus driver. As they walked down the 7th fairway in contention on Saturday, Cricket turned to Coody and asked him what time the telecast was supposed to begin.

"I don't know, Cricket," Coody said. "Why? What difference does it make?"

"Well, to tell you the truth, I didn't expect us to be doing this good," Pritchett explained. "I told my boss that my grandmother back in Texas was sick and I had to go see her. He doesn't know I'm here."

By the time they reached the 13th hole, Coody had made five birdies and had taken a three-shot lead. But Cricket wasn't taking any chances. On the 11th hole, he draped a towel over his head and put on a big, floppy hat and sunglasses.

For many years, Arnold Palmer had a caddie at the Masters who was every bit as strong-willed as Palmer himself. "Ironman" knew Palmer's game and his personality and was never intimidated by the man or his record.

In the final round of the 1960 Masters, Palmer pushed his approach to the 15th green, and the ball came to rest off the green. He hit a poor chip, leaving himself a fifteen-footer for a birdie. He tossed his club to Ironman in anger and, in return, got a very hard stare.

"He gave me just the kind of look my father used to give me when I lost my temper," Palmer remembered. "I was ashamed of myself, and I calmed down, and focused on the work I had left."

Palmer went on to par the hole, then made two birdies on the way in to edge Ken Venturi.

CONGRESSIONAL
COUNTRY CLUB

When Congressional Country Club, in the Washington suburb of Bethesda, Maryland opened for play in 1924, the future looked bright. The club had 825 lifetime members and over 600 active members. The membership was drawn not only from Washington's political and social elite but also from the top of the American business world.

Over 7,000 people jammed the club for the opening dinner dance, including President and Mrs. Coolidge, the Secretarys of State and the Treasury (just to name two) and the chief justice of the Supreme Court. No less a figure than Tommy Armour, the winner of the U.S. and British Opens and the PGA Championship, was hired as the club's first professional.

But the Great Depression soon began to take its toll on the club's fortunes. Membership dwindled. Dues were decreased. Bills went unpaid. Finally, the club was sold at auction to a group of members for a scant $270,000.

Then something good happened: World War II.

With the outbreak of the war, the Office of Strategic Services—the forerunner of the Central Intelligence Agency— needed a place near Washington to house and train recruits in the delicate arts of espionage and sabotage. Congressional, with its sprawling golf course and massive clubhouse, was perfect. Plus, it offered the added bonus of being a place where the head of the OSS, General "Wild Bill" Donovan, could entertain members of Congress over cocktails on the terrace—all the better to help insure funding for his pet projects.

Congressional—or "Area F," as it was designated—served as a OSS training ground for two-and-a-half years. At the end of that time, the government rental had allowed the club to pay off all its outstanding bills and put almost $50,000 in the bank. On top of all that, the government kicked in $187,000 to help restore the place to its earlier splendor.

Who says Washington can't do anything right?

THE CROSBY

An invitation to play in the Bing Crosby National Pro-Am—now the AT&T Pebble Beach National Pro-Am—has long been one of the most coveted items in golf. One year Maury Luxford, the tournament chairman, was in a restroom at Los Angeles International Airport when a man approached him.

"I've got $25,000 in cash in my pocket," he said. "It's yours for an invitation."

"Nope," Luxford replied.

Beginning with Bing himself, the Crosby has always attracted more than its share of show business celebrities. From Bob Hope to Phil Harris to James Garner to Jack Lemmon, the guys from Hollywood have given the tournament a special aura. Today, Bill Murray is the actor who gets most of the attention.

In 1995, when bad weather forced the cancellation of play on Saturday, CBS arranged for a celebrity shoot-out, which was won by Murray, who was dressed in bib overalls.

"I can't believe I'm going to give a check to someone dressed like you," joked AT&T chairman Bob Allen.

"And I can't believe I'm taking one from someone dressed like you," Murray replied.

Bing Crosby was a fine golfer who played in both the U.S. and British Amateurs. His son, Nathaniel, won the 1981 U.S. Amateur at San Francisco's Olympic Club under circumstances that were positively spooky.

At nineteen, Nathaniel was a very good player, but in all honesty, was not given much of a chance in a field that included players like Jay Sigel, Hal Sutton, Brad Faxon, and Willie Wood as well as many members of the Great Britain/Ireland Walker Cup team that had competed the previous week at Cypress Point.

But as so often happens in match play, the favorites faced each other in early rounds, setting up a thirty-six-hole final between Crosby and Brian Lindley—a relative unknown from southern California. Crosby was down after the morning eighteen, but fought back. As he was walking along the rough on the 7th hole in the afternoon, something happened to ABC's Bob Rosburg that made him think that Crosby just might pull it off.

"I stepped on something in the rough, bent down and picked it up, and was amazed to see that it was a pipe just like one of the pipes Bing used to have," says Rosburg. "I kind of thought, 'Geez, it's like Bing is here someplace.' I told [producer] Terry Jastrow about it. I said it was like an omen."

Sure enough, the match was even after thirty-six holes and Nathaniel ran in a long putt on the first playoff hole to win.

CYPRESS POINT GOLF CLUB

The 233-yard, par-3 16th hole at Cypress Point is one of the most treacherous and yet most beautiful holes in golf. It plays across an inlet and oftentimes into a stiff wind. Legend has it that architect Dr. Alister Mackenzie had planned the hole as a short par 4 but was persuaded to make it a par 3 by Marion Hollins, the 1921 U.S. Women's Amateur champion.

Hollins, a wealthy socialite, was one of the founding forces behind both Cypress Point and Pasatiempo Golf Club. She oversaw the construction of Cypress Point, and when she learned that Mackenzie felt the carry over the water on 16 was too severe, she set out to prove him wrong. The two went out to the proposed site for the tee. Then Hollins teed up a ball and drove it over the water to the land on the other side. The green is located where the ball landed.

Incidentally, while Pasatiempo has often been overshadowed by other great northern California courses like Cypress Point, Pebble Beach, the Olympic Club, and the San Francisco Golf Club, Mackenzie thought enough of the place that he lived in a house just off the 6th hole. When he died, his ashes were scattered over the golf course.

THE DEEPDALE
CALCUTTA SCANDAL

It's safe to say that for almost as long as people have been
playing golf, people have been betting on the outcome of
matches and tournaments. Given the power of money—especially easy money like winning a bet—it's a wonder that golf
has been so relatively scandal-free. Still, that's not to say that
the game hasn't had its sordid moments—and one of the
worst was the Deepdale Calcutta Scandal.

Deepdale is one of the most exclusive clubs on Long Island
and has been for about as long as anyone can remember. For
many years the club hosted a Calcutta tournament that drew
both good players and high rollers from up and down the East
Coast. While purists would wring their hands over the bla-
tant gambling, nobody did much about it until a huge scandal broke in 1955.

It seems that a low-handicap amateur got his hand on
another man's invitation. He and another good player entered
as a team, but claimed to have much higher handicaps than
they really did. Incredibly, no one bothered to check on either
the men or their handicaps. They wound up shooting a two-
round net score of 58-57-115, which easily won their flight
and the $45,000 pool—all for a bet of $1,900.

Inevitably, word of the team's win spread outside the cozy little world of the club and the tournament, and soon the New York press was onto the story. In the end, one of the players admitted his guilt and publicly apologized to the original invitee—whose illness opened the door for the two cheats—and refused to accept any winnings. His partner and a third coconspirator, however, split almost $20,000 in winnings. The rest of the money, which went to a group of Deepdale members who had purchased a part of the team in the Calcutta auction, was donated to charity.

If there was an upside to the scandal, it was that it gave the USGA a bully pulpit to rail publicly against gambling—and it largely put an end to Calcuttas on the scale of Deepdale's.

JIMMY DEMARET

Jimmy Demaret was watching the telecast of the 1958 Masters in the clubhouse at Augusta National. When Arnold Palmer hit his tee shot to the back of the green on the par-3 16th, Demaret said, "There's no way he gets down in two from there."

Palmer chipped in.

"See, I told you," Demaret said, laughing.

It's one of the traditions at Augusta National that all past champions are invited to play. It's a nice tradition, even though it can be a little uncomfortable watching players who can no longer handle the course.

One year Jimmy Demaret ran into one of the older past champions as he headed for the first tee.

"Play hard. I've got you in the Calcutta," he said. "I bet all my money that you'd break 90."

"I was talking to Jimmy Demaret about Augusta National one day and he was going through it hole by hole," said Dave Marr. "When he got to the second hole he called the trees down the left side the 'Ticket Counter,' because if you hit it there it was the fastest way of making sure you'd be leaving town early."

Like many professional golfers, Jimmy Demaret enlisted in the armed services during World War II. But since he served in the Special Services, he was never in much danger of encountering enemy fire. In fact, a writer once asked him how he spent the war years.

"I never got out of Shermans," he replied.

"The tanks?" the writer asked.

"No, the bar in San Diego," Jimmy said with a laugh.

There's a great sense of tradition at the Masters, in no small part because Augusta National goes out of its way to honor the players who have won the tournament. Of course, it helps that the list of winners reads like an honor roll of the game's greatest champions.

One way the club honors its supreme champions is by naming a bridge in their honor. Gene Sarazen has one. Byron Nelson has one. Ben Hogan has one, too.

Not much in this world bothered Jimmy Demaret, but seeing as he was the first three-time winner of the Masters, he sometimes wondered why he couldn't get a bridge of his own. Finally, one day he asked Clifford Roberts about it. Naturally, Jimmy being Jimmy, he put his own spin on the question.

"Cliff," he asked, "don't you think I could at least get an outhouse named after me?"

Mr. Roberts was not amused.

The role of "Elder Statesman to the Game of Golf" wasn't one that was particularly well suited to Jimmy Demaret. Still, he had infinite wisdom about the game.

At one point a writer was talking to Jimmy about some young phenom who had won a tournament just after turning pro. He may or may not have been another "next Jack Nicklaus." Either way, it didn't matter to Jimmy.

"Let's wait and see how he does when he discovers just how hard this game really is," Demaret said.

Jimmy Demaret was a player who was known to take a drink now and then. Or two. Or three if the company was good and there was no pressing business to attend to—although in the great scheme of things, there was seldom anything more important to Jimmy Demaret than spending time with his friends.

One morning he showed up at the first tee to meet his pro-am partners. Since the night before had been spent with an especially convivial group, he was more than a little worse for wear. Naturally, his partners were sympathetic, including one who told Jimmy that a particularly wicked hangover had convinced him to stop drinking ten years earlier.

"You mean when you wake up in the morning, that's as good as you're going to feel all day?" an incredulous Demaret asked.

Jimmy Demaret was paired with an unusually inept partner in a pro-am, and no matter what he suggested, it was clear the man just wasn't going to improve. Finally, in frustration and desperation, the man turned to Jimmy and asked: "Isn't there anything I can do to improve?"

"Sure, play shorter courses," Jimmy answered.

DISASTERS

Marty Fleckman was a twenty-three-year old from the University of Houston who shot a 67 in the first round of the 1967 U.S. Open at Baltusrol. While Fleckman was one of the country's top amateurs and a protégé of Byron Nelson, few people expected him to be a serious threat to win the Open. But Fleckman hung on and came back with rounds of 73 and 69. Suddenly, it appeared that an amateur might win the Open for the first time since Johnny Goodman won in 1933.

Alas, it wasn't to be. Fleckman skied to an 80 in the final round.

"I finally got back on my game," he told reporters who asked him what happened.

Ray Ainsley was a club pro from Ojai, California, who was playing along nicely in the 1938 U.S. Open at Cherry Hills—until he reached the 16th hole. Ainsley's second shot found a stream that ran in front of the green.

Ainsley carefully studied the situation and decided that he could play the ball from the water.

Bad idea. By the time he was finished he'd taken a 19, which remains a U.S. Open record for futility.

Roland Hancock was a young professional from North Carolina who found himself in a very unlikely position with just two holes left to play in the 1928 U.S. Open at Olympia Fields, outside Chicago: he was leading.

Not only was Roland Hancock leading the Open, but he could afford to bogey the last two holes and still win.

But as luck would have it, as he walked to the 17th tee, a fan yelled "Stand back. Stand back. Make way for the next U.S. Open champion!"

Roland Hancock double-bogied the 17th hole.

Roland Hancock double-bogied the 18th hole.

Roland Hancock missed joining Johnny Farrell and Bob Jones in a playoff by one stroke.

NICK FALDO

England's Nick Faldo isn't widely noted for his sense of humor, at least when he's on the golf course. Still, he managed to find some humor when he hit the ball into trouble during the 1992 U.S. Open at Pebble Beach.

He hit his ball into a tree, and the official ruled that he had to identify it in order to insure that he did, in fact, have an unplayable lie.

The only way to identify the ball, however, was for Faldo to climb up the tree. Halfway up, he asked a very Tarzanlike question.

"Where the hell is Jane?"

BRAD FAXON

Brad Faxon is an outstanding player who came out of Rhode Island, enjoyed a fine amateur career, and has become one of the most consistent players on the Tour. In 1996, he came to Augusta along with several members of his family.

Early in the week, he called his father and asked him to come over to the house he was renting and pick up his tournament badges. His father told him he'd be right over.

When Mr. Faxon arrived at the address he had written down, he went to the front door, but it was locked and no one answered his knock. He tried another door, but to no avail. Finally, he squeezed through a small door designed to let the family dog in and out.

Arriving in the house, he heard the shower running in one of the bathrooms. He sat down and was thumbing through a magazine when he heard the water stop running.

"Brad, I'm out here," he yelled. "Where are the badges?"

He heard the bathroom door open and was surprised to look up and see a soaking wet Mrs. Colin Montgomery standing in the hallway, wrapped in a towel.

"I'm very sorry," he said. "I'm Brad Faxon's father."

"Yeah, right," said a skeptical Mrs. Montgomery.

B rad Faxon and Tiger Woods were paired in one of Tiger's first tournaments as a professional. Later, writers asked Faxon about the enormous gallery that had followed his group.

"I guess they heard what a charismatic player I am," he said, laughing.

FOREIGN AFFAIRS

Australia's Peter Thomson is probably best known as the winner of five British Opens, but he was also instrumental in the growth of golf across the Pacific. As such, he's seen some things on the golf course that are . . . well, unusual.

"I was playing in Malaysia, and the tournament was plagued with terrible rain problems," he said. "It looked like the rains would never stop, so they hired a Bumoo to come in and work his particular form of magic. The man sat under a tree in the midst of the golf course, working with a handful of bones. He built a small fire, roasted some garlic, and waved the smoke around. Then, before you knew it, the rains cleared. Bumoos are very good at their craft, and quite inexpensive as well."

Incidentally, Peter Thomson has never been much for displaying the trophies he's won over his career. In fact, there is scarcely a bit of silver to be seen in his house in Melbourne. Still, during a visit to the British Open one year, his wife,

Mary, came across a company offering a replica of the British Open trophy—the old claret jug. When she tried to place an order, she was told that only former champions could purchase a copy. When she told the man her husband was a former champion, he was skeptical—even indignant.

"Really? When did he win the Open championship?" he sniffed.

"Oh, 1954, 1955, 1956, 1958, and 1965," she answered.

For much of his life, Sam Snead was an avid sportsman who loved to hunt and fish almost as much as he loved to play golf. He traveled to Africa several times on safari, and on one of these trips he was talked into playing in a tournament in Nairobi. At the very least, he figured, it would be an easy way to pick up a few thousand dollars.

You can imagine his surprise when he won the tournament and was presented with the first prize: three leopard skins.

When Americans think of Canada, they don't really think of it as a foreign country. Still, it's not like going across town for a tournament. Just ask Jackie Burke, Jr.

Burke traveled north for the Canadian Open one year. After a long drive, he checked into his hotel in Toronto. After a good night's sleep, he came down to the lobby and asked for directions to the golf course. The directions must have been very complicated.

The Canadian Open was being played in Montreal that year.

THE GREENBRIER

In the 1950s, President Dwight Eisenhower decided to build an elaborate bunker to house the surviving members of Congress in the event of a nuclear attack on Washington. He further decided that it should be built at The Greenbrier, the elegant and sprawling resort in the West Virginia mountains.

The bunker contained sleeping areas for both senators and members of the House of Representatives, meeting areas, dining facilities, and even a television studio with four different backdrops—one for each season.

Construction of the bunker—a massive project—was done in great secrecy. Still, the mammoth excavation posed a problem: what to do with the tons and tons of soil. The good people at The Greenbrier came up with a perfect solution: they built a third nine and then, just to ensure divine blessing on the entire project, they also gave some soil to a nearby Catholic church for a new parking lot.

The bunker was never used—mercifully—but its existence remained a secret for decades, until a new manager was hired by The Greenbrier. In the course of his work, he came across some bills and invoices that struck him as strange. Thinking the hotel might be getting bilked, he investigated and learned of the bunker's existence. By that time, the Cold War was largely over and the bunker had become public knowledge.

One last note about the bunker: In 1977, when Tip O'Neill was sworn in as Speaker of the House, he received a briefing about the procedures for leaving Washington in the event of a nuclear attack. At that time, he was told that the bunker would house only members of Congress. Spouses were not included.

"Well, you can stop right now," Tip said. "I'm not going without Millie."

RALPH GULDAHL

Doc Middlecoff claims that "You don't win the Open. The Open wins you." If that's true, Ralph Guldahl is a good case in point.

Guldahl, who won two Opens, a Masters, and three straight Western Opens, was the only player on the course who had a chance to catch Sam Snead and win the 1937 Open at Oakland Hills. While the pressure was enormous, Guldahl played along calmly, almost as though he were in a trance. Nothing seemed to bother him as he made four pars and two birdies over the last six holes.

On the difficult 16th hole, he hit his second shot into a greenside bunker. When he reached his ball, he saw that it had come to rest against a cigar butt. In his situation, some players might have panicked. Others would have asked for a ruling. Guldahl simply played the shot, hitting both the ball and the butt onto the green. Then he made his putt for par.

When he reached the final green he had two putts to win. Before he hit the putt, he calmly took a few seconds and combed his hair for the newsreels.

WALTER HAGEN

Walter Hagen won four British Opens and came close to winning in 1926 at Royal Lytham. He came to the final hole needing to make a two to tie Bob Jones. After hitting a good drive, Hagen sent his caddie up to the green to hold the flagstick. He didn't pull the shot off, but you wouldn't know it by the way he left town: sitting in the back of a Rolls Royce limousine, tossing golf balls to his adoring fans, who cheered him wildly.

CLAUDE HARMON

Claude Harmon, who won the 1948 Masters, was one of those rare individuals who are great players and great teachers as well—witness all the years he was the professional at Winged Foot and Seminole. His sons went on to become fine teachers as well, with Butch receiving a lot of notoriety for working with players like Greg Norman and Tiger Woods. Still, Claude wasn't all that impressed by his son's high-profile pupils.

"Hell, Butch," he told his son once. "Anybody can teach Greg Norman. He's already the best player in the world. The real challenge is teaching a bunch of your members who can barely get the ball in the air. And let me tell you something. That's where the fun is, too."

BEN HOGAN

Even when he was well past his prime as a competitor, Ben Hogan was idolized by his fellow players.

"In 1967, I was playing in a tournament at the Champions Club in Houston," remembers Tom Weiskopf. "Jeanne and I hadn't been married that long and she really didn't know that much about golf. We were sharing a house with Bert Yancey and Tony Jacklin. After Friday's round, Jeanne called to get the Saturday pairings. She called out and said I was playing with 'Al Geiberger and somebody named Ben Hogan—who's he?' We just cracked up.

"Anyway, the next day both Ben and I shot 67s, but the thing I remember is that when guys would finish their rounds they'd come out on the course to watch Ben. You never see that. Never. After I finished, I went back to the house and players began coming by. They wanted to know what it was like to play with Ben. They asked what club he hit here or what kind of shot he played there.

"Finally, Jeanne said, 'I don't know why you guys find Ben Hogan so interesting. He hits every fairway and every green. Tom is much more interesting to watch. He drives it into the trees. He hits it into the rough and the bunkers. It's a thrill a minute with Tom.'"

L ate in his playing career, Ben Hogan was paired with a young player, who was very much in awe of the Great Man. While understandably nervous, he was encouraged by his good play. When Hogan praised him following the round, it gave him just enough courage to ask Hogan a question about the golf swing.

"The answer is out there—in the dirt," Hogan said, pointing to the practice tee. "You've got to dig it out yourself."

G olf Digest once assigned Pulitzer prize–winning columnist Dave Anderson of the New York Times to ask a wide variety of golfers a simple question: "If you could play just one course for the rest of your life, which course would it be?"

Naturally, one of Dave's first calls went to Ben Hogan. Dave explained the question to Mr. Hogan's secretary, and she suggested that Dave call back in a couple of days. When he did, he got a simple answer:

"Seminole," she said.

"Did Mr. Hogan happen to say why he picked Seminole?" Dave asked, politely.

"No, Mr. Anderson, and I think you're lucky to get as much as you did," she replied.

A few days later Hogan relented, and explained that the variety of wind conditions on the seaside course in Palm Beach made the course play differently every day.

"I used to go there for a month before the Masters and play the course every day," Hogan told Anderson. "I was just as excited about playing it on the last day as I was on the day I arrived."

Privacy is very important to Ben Hogan. He respected other people's privacy and expected them to respect his as well. When someone didn't, he wasn't reluctant about letting his displeasure show.

One afternoon he was having lunch in the clubhouse at Shady Oaks when a man approached.

"Ben, I read your book [*Five Lessons of Modern Golf*], but it didn't help me very much," the man said.

"Maybe you ought to read it again," Hogan said.

On another occasion, he was having dinner with friends when a man approached their table.

"Ben, you probably don't remember me, but we played together a few years ago," the man said.

Hogan looked at the man coldly for a long moment.

"You're right," Hogan said. "I don't remember you."

Nick Faldo came to Fort Worth to visit Ben Hogan. They met for lunch at Hogan's club, Shady Oaks, and Hogan happily autographed a copy of his book, *Five Lessons of Modern Golf*, for Faldo.

In the course of lunch, Faldo asked Hogan what he needed to do to win the U.S. Open.

"Shoot the lowest score, Nick," said Hogan.

As they finished their meals, Faldo asked Hogan if he'd come out to the practice tee and watch Faldo hit some balls.

"Well, Nick, you're a fine player," said Hogan. "I might tell you something that would only confuse you. I've always believed you're better off working it out by yourself."

Faldo thanked Hogan and headed for the practice tee. Several minutes later, an employee of the Hogan company asked Ben if he wanted to go out and watch Faldo practice.

Hogan thought for a moment.

"Does Nick play our clubs?" Hogan asked.

"No," the man replied.

"Then I think I'll just sit here and finish my wine," said Hogan.

One day then–PGA Tour commissioner Deane Beman paid a courtesy call on Ben Hogan. The two sat in Hogan's office in Fort Worth and, not surprisingly, the subject turned to equipment—specifically, golf balls. Beman, a fine player in his own right, was making the case that the modern ball went so far that many of the great old courses were no longer suitable tests for championship play.

"You know, Deane, if I were playing today I'd play a Surlyn ball," Hogan said.

Beman was stunned. Balata is the cover good players favor nearly universally, or at least they did until very recently. Surlyn was considered too hard and, therefore, too lacking in feel.

"Why?" asked Beman.

"It's better," said Hogan.

"Why?" Beman asked.

"I'm not saying," said Hogan.

Ben Hogan's comeback from an almost-fatal car crash to enjoy his greatest success is the stuff of legends—and as such, it naturally attracted Hollywood's interest. The movie *Follow the Sun*, starred Glenn Ford, and it doesn't take Siskel and Ebert to realize that the film left a lot to be desired.

As you'd expect, Hogan was on-site as a technical adviser and reportedly hit all the golf shots. He was determined to make the film as accurate as possible—which led to an early battle with the studio.

Hogan arrived at Riviera Country Club, where much of the film was shot, and noticed that the irons being used were not the same year and model he'd actually used. Hogan insisted that filming stop until the correct irons were located.

The producer and director argued that no one would notice.

"I noticed," Hogan said.

They told him that the delay would cost them $100,000.

Hogan didn't care.

Filming stopped until the correct clubs could be found.

In the days following his accident, many speculated that Hogan might not survive, let alone play golf again. Apparently, Hogan never doubted he would make a comeback.

Just hours after the accident, he was visited by a fellow player, Herman Keiser, the 1946 Masters champion. Hogan asked Keiser to do him a favor.

"Herman, will you check on my clubs for me?" he asked.

It's said that nobody ever practiced harder than Ben Hogan, but nobody understood more clearly the difference between practice and just beating balls—as a young player found out when he approached Hogan and told him how hard he'd been working on his game.

"You might as well be doing push-ups," Hogan said.

Ken Venturi carries in his wallet a quote from Ben Hogan: "For every day I miss practicing it takes me two days to get back to where I was."

Several years ago, in an interview for CBS Sports, Venturi asked Hogan why he practiced so long and so hard.

"I had to," Hogan said. "My swing was so bad."

"Is that the only reason?" Venturi asked, sensing the answer beforehand.

"No, I loved it. There's nothing I loved more than waking up in the morning and knowing I could head for the course to practice. I always got the most pleasure out of improving."

"I remember playing down in Houston one year and one of the rounds was rained out," says Jay Hebert, the 1960 PGA champion. "Most of the guys left the course, and as I was getting ready to leave I heard this *thwack, thwack, thwack*. I went around the corner and there was Ben practicing in the pouring rain. He'd gone inside a tent, rolled up one of the sides, and was hitting balls to his caddie. There wasn't another player in the world who would do that."

"I went down to the Ryder Cup matches in 1967 in Houston," recalled the late Bob Drum. "Hogan was captain, and everyone figured the American team would win easily. But for some reason Ben got kinda mad with Arnold [Palmer]. Arnold was playing a practice round, and he asked Hogan if he had any of the small British balls he could practice with. Hogan sort of glared at him.

"'Didn't you bring any?' he asked Arnold, who told him he didn't, because he thought they were being supplied by the PGA.

"'Well, I'm glad you at least remembered to bring your clubs,' Hogan said, and then drove off in his cart.

"I don't know if he was trying to psych Arnold up or what, but if he was, it worked," said Drummer. "Arnold went out and won all five of his matches."

Lanny Wadkins often played with Ben Hogan when he first came out on tour. In fact, he still has an uncashed check that Hogan wrote to settle up after one match. While Hogan enjoyed playing with younger players, there was never a lot of joking around on the course.

"I remember one match when I was kidding around with the other players in the foursome," Wadkins said. "Hogan looked over at me and said, 'I don't play jolly golf.' That was the end of the jolly golf for the day."

Claude Harmon was one of Ben Hogan's closest friends on tour. Hogan admired his playing ability but also appreciated his sense of humor.

Harmon and Hogan were paired together one year at the Masters. Harmon made a hole-in-one on the difficult 12th hole. The crowd went crazy, but Hogan's reaction was notably restrained.

"It kind of bothered my father, because he and Ben were such good friends," recalls Bill Harmon, the professional at Newport (Rhode Island) Country Club. Either that night or the following night my parents went out for dinner with Ben and Valerie. They had a couple of cocktails before dinner, and my father said, 'You know, Ben, you didn't say much when I made that ace.'"

"Hogan thought for a second, then said, 'You know, Claude, your hole-in-one didn't help me one damn bit.'"

Ben Hogan and Byron Nelson first met as youngsters when they caddied at Glen Garden Golf Club in Fort Worth. In fact, Nelson edged Hogan in a playoff for the caddie championship one year—setting the stage for a rivalry that would continue through the years.

In 1945, Nelson had a remarkable year. He won eleven tournaments in a row, eighteen tournaments in all. While Hogan played in some of the tournaments, much of his time was spent in the service.

When he was finally discharged, he traveled to Oregon for the Portland Open. By this time newspapers and magazines had taken to calling Nelson "Mr. Golf"—which, no doubt, embarrassed the modest Nelson as much as it annoyed Hogan.

Hogan was more determined than usual in Portland. He shot a record 261, which easily won the tournament and was fourteen strokes better than Nelson. As he walked off the final green, his old friend Jimmy Demaret congratulated him.

"I hope that takes care of this 'Mr. Golf' business," Hogan said grimly.

Demaret and Hogan were paired in a tournament, and Demaret looked on as Hogan birdied ten holes on the way to a 64. Later, after a lengthy and pleasant visit to the clubhouse, Demaret was heading for his car when he saw Hogan out on the practice tee. Demaret strolled over.

"What the hell are you doing, Ben?" he asked.

"Practicing," Hogan said.

"I know that, but why?" Demaret said.

"Because there's no reason in the world a man can't birdie every hole, and I want to be the one to do it," he answered.

"Ben was wonderful to be paired with," remembers five-time British Open champion Peter Thomson. "Unlike some great players, he never felt the need to strut the stage. He played his game and was quite content to let you play yours. I remember one time when my mate Kel Nagle was playing with Ben. Naturally, the gallery was quite large, and when Kel holed a 2-iron for a hole-in-one, they let out quite a roar. Ben just looked over and said, 'Nice shot.'

"Another time, Kel was paired with Ben at Colonial. Kel one-putted the first five greens and then on the 6th hole his ball came to rest against a greenside bunker. All he could do was putt the ball left-handed from some twenty feet away. When that putt went in as well, he looked over at Ben almost apologetically. Hogan just broke up with laughter."

On another occasion, Hogan was paired with Charlie Coe, the great amateur from Oklahoma, at Colonial. On the first few holes, Coe—who was understandably nervous—complimented Hogan on his fine shotmaking.

Hogan never said a word.

Coe continued to praise Hogan's good shots, to no avail. Finally, Coe gave up and concentrated on his game. It wasn't until the 15th hole when Hogan spoke to Coe.

"Charlie, do you have a cigarette?" he asked.

That was it. The total conversation between the two men during their round. But later, in the locker room, Hogan approached Coe and said something he'd never forget.

"Charlie, I really enjoyed playing with you today. That was the most enjoyable round I think I've ever played."

Paul Harney, who won seven times on the PGA Tour, idolized Ben Hogan. So you can imagine how unnerved he was when, on his first trip to the Colonial, Hogan approached him on the putting green and invited Harney to join him for a practice round.

"I was so nervous I almost said, 'No, thanks.' But instead I went out and parred the first hole," Harney recalled years later. "That was the only par I made all day. By the time we finished I felt like dirt. I just felt awful. The next morning, I was eating breakfast in the clubhouse when Ben walked by and asked me if I wanted to play another practice round. I did, and parred the first hole. I didn't make another par until the 18th. As we walked off the final green, Ben said, 'Well, son, at least you improved.'"

On another occasion, Ben Hogan invited a young player to join him for a practice round. After several holes, he noticed the rookie was paying particularly close attention to Hogan's club selection. Finally, when they reached a par 3, Hogan gave him a bit of advice—and a lesson.

"Son, don't ever go by someone else's club selection out here," he said. "It's too easy to get fooled. I'll show you."

With that, he pulled out a 6-iron and hit it pin high. He took a second ball from his caddie and hit the 6-iron over the green, ten yards past his first ball. Then he took a third ball and dead-handed it, leaving it ten yards short of the first ball. Three seemingly identical swings. Three different distances.

Throughout his career, Ben Hogan played by sight instead of yardage—as did most players of his time. But this was difficult on a course with blind shots, like the National Golf Links on Long Island. Hogan came to the course to play with some business associates, and he was given a local caddie who was legendary for his ability to hand a player the right club.

On one hole, Hogan asked the caddie how far he had to the green.

"An easy eight," said the caddie.

"No, I asked how far," Hogan replied.

"Just an easy eight," said the caddie.

Hogan gave him a withering glare, then pulled a club from his bag.

It wasn't an 8-iron. And he hit it stiff.

Of all Ben Hogan's great wins, surely his triumph in the 1951 U.S. Open at Oakland Hills would rank as one of his greatest. His final-round 67 over the brutally punishing course was so remarkable that it prompted South Africa's Bobby Locke to wonder: "Did Ben play every hole?"

If it's true that timing is everything in life, the people who were running the Hershey Country Club in 1951 had about as bad a sense of timing as is humanly possible.

On the eve of the final two rounds of the U.S. Open at Oakland Hills, they announced that after ten years they wouldn't be renewing Hershey's contract with Ben Hogan.

After Hogan's final-round 67 clinched the championship, a writer asked him if it could possibly be true that he wouldn't be returning to Hershey.

"Yes," he said, grinning. "So if you know of a good club job, let me know. I'll take it."

Later, sitting in the locker room at Oakland Hills, he was approached by Clayton Heafner, who shot a final-round 69 to finish second. Heafner congratulated Hogan on his win.

"Thank you, Clayton," Hogan said. "How'd you do?"

Very few sequence photographs of Hogan's swing exist, and for a very good reason: Ben Hogan didn't want to be bothered.

"I remember going out to a practice tee with a little camera early in my career," remembers Bob Toski, the fine teacher and player. "I stood behind Ben and started to take pictures while he practiced. I couldn't have taken more than two shots when Ben turned around and glared—which was a look you didn't forget.

"'Oh, it's you, Bob,' Hogan said, raking over another ball. 'It's okay.'"

Leonard Kamsler, the veteran *Golf* magazine photographer, wasn't as lucky.

"I was assigned to take some sequence photos of him down at a tournament in Texas," recalls Kamsler. "It was a big, bulky, noisy camera, so I couldn't take it out onto the course. Every day I waited around the practice tee looking for Hogan, but he never showed up. Finally, one of the guys in the golf shop tipped me off that Ben warmed up on an adjacent course. The next day, I headed over there about an hour before his starting time. He saw me coming, lugging this camera. He watched me for a minute or so, then put the club back in the bag, called his caddie in, and left."

Some of the finest films of Hogan's swing were owned by the late Tony Ravielli, a talented artist who did the illustrations for Hogan's 1957 classic instruction book, *Five Lessons of Modern Golf*, which was coauthored with Herbert Warren Wind, who was then a writer for the fledgling *Sports Illustrated*.

Ravielli used an illustration technique that he'd used successfully in work for medical textbooks. To ensure that the drawings were as anatomically accurate as possible, Hogan was filmed wearing shorts and a T-shirt. The results were drawings that were clear, precise, and dramatic.

The book is widely regarded—even forty years after its publication—as one of the finest books of golf instruction ever written. The irony is, it came about almost by accident.

Hogan had agreed to do a piece for a 1955 issue of *Life* magazine titled "Hogan's Secret." A short while later, *Life*'s sister publication, *Sports Illustrated*, ran some of the drawings—without Hogan's permission. Hogan threatened to sue. Time-Life founder Henry Luce intervened and agreed to pay Hogan for the drawings. He then suggested that the article be expanded into book form—and a classic was born.

B en Hogan's course management and shotmaking were so precise that they left his fellow players in awe.

"I watched Ben play his first two rounds at Oakland Hills in the '51 Open and I thought he was the luckiest player I'd ever seen," one player said. "He never had an awkward lie. He was always playing from a level spot in the fairway, while everyone else was getting these funny lies. But after the second round, I realized there was no luck involved. He was that good."

A nother example of Hogan's brilliance as a shotmaker came from his play in the 1954 U.S. Open at Baltusrol Golf Club. His caddie was Billy Farrell, the young son of Baltusrol's pro and the 1928 U.S. Open Champion, Johnny Farrell. Billy would later turn pro, played the Tour for many years, and is the longtime professional at The Stanwich Club in Greenwich, Connecticut.

"Even as a kid I knew what a great shotmaker Hogan was," Billy remembers. "Everybody who played golf knew about Hogan. But it wasn't until I caddied for him at the Open that I really appreciated just how good he really was. In the final round he hit his drive on the 11th hole. When we got to the ball, I noticed that it was next to a series of three divots— the divots Hogan took in the first three rounds. That's when I realized how good perfection really is."

After his final round at the 1951 Open, Hogan was congratulated by Ione Jones, the wife of architect Robert Trent Jones, who had made numerous controversial revisions to the course prior to the Open. Hogan thanked her and then let her know his opinion of her husband's work.

"If your husband had to play his courses for a living, you'd be in a breadline," he said.

Few players in history ever read a golf course as well as Ben Hogan. He could arrive at a tournament, play a practice round, and judge what the winning score would be with uncanny accuracy. He knew the holes he could expect to birdie, those where par was a good score, and those that presented the most danger.

The final round of the 1953 British Open at Carnoustie provided an interesting glimpse into how Hogan's mind worked in the closing stages of a championship.

With Roberto de Vicenzo shooting himself out of contention with a closing-round 73, Hogan's only concern was Antonio Cerda. After playing the 15th hole, Hogan asked his friend broadcaster John Derr how Cerda stood.

"He's 3-under through 13," Derr told Hogan, who knew he led by two strokes as he faced the long, par-3 16th.

Hogan's tee shot stopped within ten feet of the hole.

Hogan walked over to the side of the tee, took a drag on his cigarette, and whispered to Derr.

"You can go get ready for your broadcast, John," he said. "This championship is all over."

Sports marketing was still in its relative infancy in the early 1950s, but that's not to say that smart businessmen didn't understand the value of associating their products with a player like Ben Hogan—and that extended well past clubs and balls, as he learned on the eve of the 1953 British Open.

Hogan had never played in the British Open, and one day he was asking a writer friend about the weather conditions in Scotland. The friend warned Hogan that it could get very cold, even in midsummer, and advised him to bring a couple pairs of long underwear. Word soon spread that Hogan was in search of some cashmere long johns, and he was contacted by New York's Abercrombie & Fitch, informing him that they had just the thing—at almost $100 a pair.

Hogan ordered two pairs.

Not to be outdone, a Fort Worth department store immediately sent him two pairs of their finest, followed by BVD, which sent him three pairs.

If nothing else, Ben Hogan would be the warmest player at Carnoustie.

During his playing days, Ben Hogan always had a keen appreciation for history. Following his win in the 1953 British Open, he was being interviewed by American radio announcer John Derr. Following the interview, Derr asked Hogan if he could have the ball he holed out with on the final green for presentation to the United States Golf Association's museum. Hogan told him to see his caddie, Cecil Timms.

"Here's the ball we won with, sir," Timms said, handing Derr a Titleist #2. "And here's the one we made the 2 with on 13. Mr. Hogan thought you'd like it for yourself."

For all the talk about Hogan being an aloof loner, there's more than enough evidence that he was generous and loyal to his friends.

In the course of one tournament, a fellow player hooked up—so to speak—with a woman of negotiable virtue. When he tried to pay her $20 for her efforts, she threatened to blackmail him. Her price was $1,000, considerably more than the player had. And there was no doubting that she would make good on her threat.

When Hogan heard about the man's problem, he quietly took the player aside and pressed ten $100 bills into his hand.

"Don't say anything to anyone," Hogan said. "And just pay me back when you can."

Ben Hogan was a man of his word—a quality he admired in others.

"By 1958, I had won ten tournaments on the Tour," remembers Ken Venturi. "I was playing MacGregor Byron Nelson irons and Titleist balls. Ben knew I wouldn't switch irons, but he said that if I ever decided to switch balls he'd like a shot at offering me a ball deal. At that time, U.S. Rubber was making both the Royal ball and the Hogan ball, and John Sproul, who was the head of U.S. Rubber, came out to San Francisco and offered me a contract to play the Royal ball. It was worth five times what Ben could offer, plus bonuses.

"I told John I'd play his ball but I needed to call Ben before I signed the contract. I called Fort Worth, but Ben was out of town until the next day. John said he had to catch a flight. He wanted me to sign the contract and call Ben later. I told him I'd given Ben my word and that was that. He got pretty upset and said I was going to blow the deal. I didn't care. Ben had been awfully good to me when I came out on tour, and if keeping my word meant blowing the deal, so be it.

"Anyway, the next day we called Ben. I told him what the offer was and he said he couldn't match it. He thanked me for calling and was about to hang up when John told him what had happened the day before. Ben asked John to put me back on the phone.

"'Ken,' he said. 'If there's ever anything you want or need, call me. I won't forget this.' And he never did."

Years later, when Hogan was in his eighties and suffering from a variety of illnesses, Ken Venturi paid a visit to his old friend. As he was leaving, he hugged Hogan and said, "I love you, Ben."

"You're not so bad yourself," Hogan quipped.

"The so-called yips got to Ben, just like they get to everyone sooner or later," says Sam Snead. "Toward the end of his career he could still hit the ball about as good as ever, but he got so he couldn't even pull the putter back from the ball. He'd stand there and smoke a whole cigarette while he looked over a putt, but then he'd freeze over the ball. Hell, in one tournament he three-putted seven greens and four-putted another. When he was playing with friends back home, they'd play 'Greenies.' You'd get points for hitting greens, but there'd be no putting."

After retiring from competition, Hogan loved to go to his club, Shady Oaks, to practice and occasionally play with a group of friends. While they admired and respected Hogan, they weren't above trying to give him the needle during their matches. And Hogan responded in kind.

Always meticulous in his preparation for the matches, Hogan left nothing to chance. It wasn't an accident that on the days Hogan and his friends played, an unusually high percentage of the flags were tucked on the right side of the greens—making it easier for Hogan to fade the ball at the holes.

Hogan loved to play at Seminole, and in fact was a member of the club. He particularly enjoyed playing in the annual pro-am tournament that the club hosted for many years.

One year a small controversy broke out when a young pro criticized the course in a local newspaper. Hogan took the man aside and sternly gave him a piece of advice.

"You listen to me," he said, his blue eyes flashing with anger. "You are a guest at every single course you play. You need them more than they need you, so you should count your blessings. If you can't bring yourself to say something nice about a course, just say, 'It's the best course of its type I've ever seen' and leave it at that. You won't be lying, and you'll be long gone before anyone tries to figure out exactly what you meant."

HOLES-IN-ONE

How's this for a weird one? A guy named Otis Guernsey hit his tee shot on the 9th hole at the Apawamis Club in Rye, New York. Unfortunately for Mr. Guernsey, he hit it badly. Very badly. In fact, he hit a wicked shank that flew across the street and landed on the 11th green of Green Meadow, a neighboring course. The ball rolled into the hole for a course-to-course ace. It was a town-to-town ace, as well. Green Meadow is in the town of Harrison.

HUSBANDS AND WIVES
(AND SIGNIFICANT OTHERS)

Want a recipe for domestic misery? Want to all but guarantee that your marriage will be whistling south faster than Amtrak's "Sunshine Special"? Have your wife caddie for you. Or worse yet, if you play in the LPGA Tour, sign up your husband. Or boyfriend. The historic landscape is littered with relationships that were shattered on the shoals of the player-caddie/wife-husband team.

Just ask Amy Alcott.

"The funniest thing I ever saw on the golf course involved a player whose husband caddied for her when she first came out on tour," Amy recalls. "It was in the late '70s. We were playing in Dallas, and the woman was in contention going into the final round. She got off to a terrible start and couldn't recover. By the time we made the turn she was 6 over, she was history, and she and her husband were barely talking. We got to the 10th hole, which was a par 3, and there was a 5-wood and a 3-iron resting against the bench where her husband had left them. Up by the green was a pitching wedge and her putter. But no husband. The next hole was a par 4. He left her driver on the tee, and her 5- and 6-irons down in the rough near the landing area. He left her sand wedge up by the green, since he was sure she'd hit it into a bunker. On the next hole, he left her 3-wood on the tee and her 4-iron in the left rough, where he was sure she was going to hook the ball. By the time we reached the 13th hole, he was pretty sure she had all the clubs she'd need, but just to be on the safe side he left her 9-iron on the tee. Now she's carrying eleven clubs. She's so mad she can barely see straight, and it's all I can do to keep from falling down laughing. We finished the hole and he was waiting on the tee. I don't think they said a word to each other for the rest of the round. It wasn't too long before they decided he'd retire from caddying—at least for her. It probably saved their marriage."

Want to know the record for futility as well as patience? It's 166 strokes—on a single hole—and it belongs to a woman who was playing in the 1912 Shawnee (Pennsylvania) Invitational. She hit her tee shot on the 130-yard, par-3 16th into the Binniekill River. As she watched the ball cascade down the rock-strewn waters, her husband urged her to jump in a nearby rowboat. As he rowed, she tried valiantly to hit the ball back to shore. With her husband cheering her on, she finally succeeded. Unfortunately, she was about a mile downstream. Not to be deterred, she played back through the woods—counting every single, miserable, humiliating stroke. Finally, she holed out—166 strokes later.

IRELAND

The American Ireland Fund is a wonderful and very worthy organization that raises money in America to help fund charities and scholarships in Ireland, as well as promote political reconciliation and economic development in the six counties. As you might imagine, the fund is supported by Irish-American leaders in the political, business, and cultural communities—people who gather at a series of fundraising dinners in cities across the country every year.

At a dinner in Boston, a speaker told the story about a hugely successful Texas rancher who traveled to Ireland to visit his ancestral home and play a little golf.

In the course of his round at Portmarnock, his caddie asked him about Texas—a place that had always captured his imagination.

"Boy, I get in my car when the sun comes up and I start driving," the Texan boasted. "By the time the sun sets in the west, I still haven't reached the end of my property."

The caddie wrapped a sympathetic arm across the Texan's shoulder.

"Don't feel badly, sir," he said. "I had a car like that once myself."

BOBBY JONES

A writer once asked Gene Sarazen what it was like to be paired with Bob Jones. Sarazen, as fierce a competitor as anyone who ever played the game, smiled warmly and said, "Bob was a wonderful man to be partnered with in a tournament, no matter how big or small. He went out of his way to make you feel like a friend—and you were."

Like many golfers, Bobby Jones was something of a loner. While he accepted being a celebrity, he very much treasured his privacy. One day a friend asked him if he liked people.

"Yes, I do," Jones replied. "But I like most people in small doses."

Bobby Jones was born and raised in Atlanta, but he was a sickly child, unable to eat solid foods until he was five years old. In fact, as a boy he was so frail that his parents were hesitant to let him play contact sports and steered him to golf.

The professional at East Lake was Stewart Maiden, an extremely serious Scot of few words. He took a liking to Bobby Jones and encouraged his interest in golf.

One of his first bits of advice to Jones was to "hit the ball hard, boy. They always come down someplace."

But when he told Jones to hit the ball hard, he didn't mean for him to swing fast—as Jones learned at the 1925 U.S. Open at Worcester (Massachusetts) Country Club. Jones was playing badly coming into the tournament and summoned Maiden to come and help. Maiden arrived, watched Jones hit a few shots, and succinctly summed up the problem.

"Why don't you hit the ball with your backswing," he said. "It's fast enough."

On another occasion, someone asked Jones about Maiden's philosophy of the game.

"It's very simple," Jones said. "Keep hitting the ball toward the hole until you get it close enough to hit it in the hole."

One year at the Masters, some players were complaining about how difficult it was to make birdies on certain of the holes.

"I don't agree with that and, frankly, don't understand it," Jones confided to a friend. "If you apply the proper imagination and strike the ball properly, you might get close enough to reasonably expect to make a birdie. That is all the course owes you."

For all his celebrity—and it was considerable—Jones never lost his ability to laugh at himself. Indeed, one of his favorite stories was about his performance at the 1926 British Open at Royal Lytham.

At that time, the final two rounds were played on Saturday. After his morning round, Jones returned to his hotel for lunch. When he returned to the course, the man who was arguably the most celebrated golfer in the field was stopped at the gate by a guard who didn't know Bob Jones from Joe Blow but did know he didn't have either a player's badge or a ticket. So Jones did what would be all but unthinkable today: he stood in line, purchased a ticket, and went on to win the first of his three British Opens.

Bobby Jones was named after his paternal grandfather, who was a deeply religious man. While he was proud of his grandson's accomplishments, he never quite got used to his playing a game on the Sabbath.

"Well, Bob, if you have to play on Sunday, do me a favor and at least make sure you play well," he said.

Bobby Jones had a wonderful education. He had a degree in mechanical engineering from Georgia Tech and a degree in English literature from Harvard. He studied law at Emory University, and absorbed it so easily that he dropped out of school and still passed the law boards. But for all his varied interests, Jones particularly loved the classics.

"The day before the start of the 1923 U.S. Amateur, nobody could find him," recalled the late Charlie Price. "It turned out he was off by himself reading Papini's *Life of Christ*."

Bobby Jones was very close to his father, the Colonel. The elder Jones wasn't all that much of a golfer, but he had a deep love for the game and a fine sense of humor.

In one of the early Masters, his son asked him to serve as a rules official. A player hit his ball into what he believed was casual water. He motioned the Colonel over and asked for a ruling.

"How do you stand?" the Colonel asked.

"Eighteen over," the player responded.

"Well, what the hell does it matter?" the Colonel said. "Take a drop or tee it up on a peg, for all I care."

It is difficult today to appreciate just what a hugely popular figure Jones was. In the "Golden Age of American Sports," as his time was known, he was its brightest star—a fact made all the more remarkable by how few Americans played the game.

In 1926, when Jones won the first of his three British Opens, he was given a ticker tape parade down Broadway.

Four years later, when he returned to New York after winning both the British Open and Amateur and having captained the winning Walker Cup team, the city of New York again turned out to honor him with a parade.

Jones was, at heart, a reluctant hero, and the adulation made him uncomfortable. His discomfort was increased by the stifling heat and humidity of July in the city.

Years later, he overheard a New York City policeman tell about the afternoon he spent sweltering in New York marching in a parade for "some golfer from down south."

"As grateful as I was for the honor," Jones said to the man, "I was suffering just as much as you were that day."

Jones was the supreme champion and easily the greatest amateur golfer in history. But upon his retirement from competitive play he realized that the time had come to earn some money. He designed a set of clubs for Spalding and agreed to make a series of twelve one-reel films for Warner Brothers. The studio paid him an astonishing $120,000 plus a percentage of the gross for the movies, which became hugely successful. It is a testimonial to Jones's popularity that some 35 million people are estimated to have seen the movies—at a time when just a fraction of that many people played the game.

After completing the Grand Slam in 1930, Jones returned to Atlanta. At a dinner in his honor, he spoke from the heart about what it meant to him to put the pressures of championship golf behind him and come home.

"I'm glad, mighty glad, to be home," he said. "To me, the best part of playing in tournaments has always been coming back home. It's going to be awfully hard to get me out of town again."

Following his retirement from competition, Jones and his friend, Clifford Roberts, a New York investment banker, set out to build the Augusta National Golf Club. Jones chose a Scottish architect, Dr. Alister Mackenzie, to help him design the course. Not surprisingly, given their affection for the Old Course at St. Andrews, Augusta National had a similar strategic feel to it.

"It's difficult to fully explain how important Bob's suggestions were," Mackenzie said later. "He constantly stressed that, to him, while a poor shot should be punished, a player should have a realistic chance of saving par. The possibility of an exceptional recovery shot should not be negated by a purely punitive hazard."

One can only wonder what he would have thought about holes such as the par-3 17th—the Island Hole—at The Players Club at Sawgrass.

In 1945, Jones asked architect Robert Trent Jones to become involved in a new course he was planning in Atlanta called Peachtree. Trent wondered if raising the necessary funds would be a problem. He was assured that it wouldn't be.

Several days later, Bobby Jones arranged a lunch for a dozen or so wealthy Atlanta businessmen.

"Fellows, it's gotten so that it takes five or six hours to play a round at East Lake, and that's not my idea of golf," Jones said. "Some of us think we need a new course in town, and we've already picked out the property. Trent here is going to help us design it. What we need from you is $100,000 each by next week."

He got it, without any questions asked.

One of Bobby Jones's closest friends was O. B. Keeler, the Atlanta newspaperman who chronicled Jones's career. Keeler knew better than most the effects the pressures of championship competition had on Jones. He knew that after winning the British Amateur and Open and the U.S. Open in 1930, the twenty-eight-year-old Jones was contemplating his retirement from competition.

In the locker room after winning the U.S. Open at Interlachen, Jones was asked by a writer what he'd do when he retired.

"You'd better tell them, O.B.," Jones said to his friend.

Keeler climbed upon a bench and quoted the English poet Hilaire Belloc:

"If I ever become a rich man
Or if I ever grow to be old,
I will build a house with a deep thatch
To shelter me from the cold,
I will hold my house in the high woods
Within a walk of the sea,
And the men that were boys when I was a boy
Shall sit and drink with me."

When Jones retired after winning the U.S. Amateur at Merion to complete his "Grand Slam," Keeler summed up his feelings for his friend:

"And now it was good-bye to golf. And I could still say what I said to people all over the world: that Bobby Jones was a much finer young man than he was a golfer. Wholly lacking in affectation, modest to the degree of shyness, generous and thoughtful of his opponents, it is not likely that his equal will come again."

Bobby Jones died in 1971, and a memorial service was held in May of the following year at the Holy Trinity Church in St. Andrews.

Jones, who was revered in Scotland, was remembered as a person who "never lost any of the values that make up the complete man: humanity, humor, consideration, and courtesy to all about him."

GUNBY JORDAN

The late Gunby Jordan was the longtime chairman of the Southern Open, a tournament he resurrected in the early 1970s. Gunby came from a wealthy southern family and attended Yale, where he became good friends with the esteemed writer Herbert Warren Wind.

For twenty years the Southern Open was played at the Green Island Country Club in Gunby's hometown, Columbus, Georgia. Gunby was a fine golfer, and he enjoyed the company of other golfers. One of his favorites was Jerry Pate, who won the Southern Open twice.

One year Jerry and a fellow player were walking down a fairway when Gunby drove up in a cart and visited with the players for a while before driving away.

"Who does that guy think he is?" the player asked Pate. "Only the officials are supposed to have carts."

"See this course?" Pate replied. "Gunby owns it. You know the bank in town? He owns that, too. Along with most of the buildings and a whole lot of the land around here. In fact, he owns about everything worth owning around here, so I guess if he wants to drive around in a cart, that's just fine."

As a boy, Gunby spent much of his time playing golf, usually in the company of caddies who were both poor and black. He developed a tremendous affection for them, and in 1986 decided he wanted to write a book about caddies. He sent out mailings to the hundreds of friends he had in the game asking for stories about caddies. He put advertisements in golf magazines soliciting material. Once he had amassed four large notebooks stuffed with anecdotes, he asked Herb Wind to help him find a writer. Herb recommended me, and it was a joyous collaboration.

After talking on the phone, Gunby decided that we should meet, and what better place than the U.S. Amateur being played at Shoal Creek in Birmingham, Alabama. The negotiations—such as they were—for my fee would be conducted over dinner. Of course, dinner would be preceded by cocktails. After regaling me with stories and assuring me that this book was going to be a bestseller, he got down to business. Gunby was an enormous man, easily 6'3" tall, and imposing, with thick black hair and bushy eyebrows that fairly leapt up and down behind his glasses—which always seemed slightly askew. He had a thick southern accent and laughed loudly and easily. He was a delight.

As we waited for the first course to arrive, he leaned toward me—much in the manner of Lyndon Johnson—and drawled, "Now, boy, how much money d'you want to write my book for me?"

I gave him a figure.

"That sounds just fine," he said, reaching for his checkbook. "I'll give you half now and half when we get it finished."

I told him that would be great, and asked if he wanted me to sign a contract.

"Hell no," he said. "If you're a friend of Herb Wind, that's good enough for me."

We finished the book a few months later, and Gunby decided he wanted to give copies as pro-am gifts for the Southern Open. Since he couldn't find a publisher that could get the book done as quickly as he wanted, Gunby did what came naturally to him: he started his own publishing company. Whatever books didn't sell became gifts at the Southern Open for years to come.

Gunby and his wife, Helen, traveled to New York City every fall for the opening of the opera season—another one of Gunby's passions. In 1987, following publication of his book, he invited Herb Wind and me to join them for lunch at the Yale Club. Gunby ordered a martini—and ruefully announced that Helen had limited him to just one drink. It wasn't long after he'd finished his martini that it became clear that he was trying to figure out how to get around his wife's edict. Finally, his eyes brightened and he motioned for the waiter.

"You know, Herb, this club's gone to hell in a handbasket," he said with feigned outrage. "Just look how puny these drinks are. You'd get more in a thimble. Surely you'll have another?"

Helen just shook her head and laughed.

PRESIDENT
JOHN F. KENNEDY

President Kennedy played a lot of his golf at the Hyannis-port Country Club, where Tom Niblet was the professional. Niblet has fond memories of the late president.

"One day he came off the course and he was unhappy about the way he played," Niblet remembers. "He asked if he could come by for a lesson. The next morning, I noticed a lot of helicopters landing. There were generals all over the place. The President called and said that something had come up and he'd have to cancel his lesson. It turns out the something that came up was a crisis in Laos—but he was still thoughtful enough to call me."

Jack Kennedy was a naturally gifted athlete, and by all accounts the best golfer to ever serve as President. Still, when he ran for the office he went to great lengths to contrast himself with President Dwight Eisenhower. To that end, he went to great lengths to hide his love for the game.

One afternoon, late in the campaign, he took a few hours out to play Cypress Point with his old friend, Paul Fay Jr. On the par-3 15th hole, Kennedy hit a shot that covered the flag all the way.

Fay urged the ball to go into the cup. Kennedy kept saying, "No, no, no."

The ball hit the cup and ended up just inches from the hole.

"You want the ball to go in the hole and I'm watching my career pass before my eyes," Kennedy joked to Fay. "If that ball had gone in the hole, the press would know in a couple hours and I'd be history."

BOBBY LOCKE

South Africa's Bobby Locke, who won four British Opens, was a brilliant if unconventional player.

"Bobby would hook everything," recalls Sam Snead. "It didn't matter how a hole played or where a pin was cut, he'd figure out a way to hook the ball into position. Of course, it didn't hurt that he might have been the greatest putter who ever lived—and he even hooked his putts. I played a two-week series of exhibitions with him in South Africa, and he didn't three-putt once. And those greens were all grain. They were impossible to read, let alone putt. I just left there shaking my head. I'd never seen anyone putt like Bobby. When we finished the exhibition, he asked me if I thought he should give the U.S. Tour a try. I looked at him and said, 'Are you kidding? Anyone who can putt like that can win anywhere.'"

So Locke came to America, and although he played for only a short time, it wasn't for lack of confidence. He would routinely bet on himself—sometimes as much as $500 per tournament.

DAVIS LOVE JR.

Davis Love Jr. was one of America's most-respected teaching professionals until his death in 1988. He was knowledgeable and patient, much in the manner of his former coach, Harvey Penick. He could also be spectacularly absent-minded, as his son Davis Love III remembers fondly.

"One time dad had to go to Spain to teach in a golf school," Davis says. "He was late for his flight so he raced to the airport in Jacksonville. He got to the curb, leaped out of the car, and checked his bags with just a few minutes to spare.

"When he returned from Spain he couldn't find his car. He was sure it had either been stolen or towed. He found a policeman and said that his car had been taken.

"'Was it a yellow Lincoln?'" the policeman asked, patiently.

"'Yes,' my father said.

"'You left it at the curb with the engine running,' the policeman said."

DAVE MARR

The 1984 U.S. Open at Winged Foot produced a popular
champion in Fuzzy Zoeller, who beat Greg Norman in a
playoff. But all week the tournament had been marred with
traffic and parking problems. So you can imagine their relief
when ABC announcers Dave Marr and Jack Whitaker arrived
at the course for the playoff on Monday. The press parking
lot was already filling up, but the adjacent players' lot was virtually empty. There were just two cars in the lot: Zoeller's and
Norman's.

Marr asked the security guard if they could park in the
players' lot.

"Sorry, Mr. Marr," the guard said, "that's for players only."

BILLY MARTIN

In 1974, when Billy Martin was managing the Texas Rangers baseball team, the club's owner, Bradford G. Corbett, arranged for Martin to join Shady Oaks Country Club.

People who knew Martin were sure Corbett had lost his mind. They might have been right.

It wasn't long before Martin committed about as bad a mistake as you could make at Shady Oaks: he, along with his best friend, Mickey Mantle, ran afoul of the club's most revered member—Ben Hogan—and Martin was asked to leave the club.

A month or so later, he was going through his mail in the Rangers' clubhouse when he got his final bar bill from Shady Oaks.

"How do they expect me to pay this?" Martin asked a friend.

"Do you need some money?" the friend asked.

"Hell no." Martin laughed. "But they won't let me back on the grounds."

DR. CARY MIDDLECOFF

Sometimes even the best players have certain holes they just can't seem to play. No matter what they try, they just never seem comfortable. The 5th hole at Colonial, a 466-yard par 4 guarded down the right side by the Trinity River, was a hole that always gave Doc Middlecoff problems. Then one year he came in from a practice round and told the writers he'd figured out how to break the jinx the hole had on him.

"First I stand on the tee and throw two new balls into the river," said Doc. "Then I throw up. Then I hit a ball into the river. It's like a peace offering."

YOUNG TOM MORRIS

The son of St. Andrews professional Old Tom Morris, Young Tom exists as a legendary—and tragic—figure in the game.

Born in 1851, he won the first of his four straight British Opens in 1868. His father also won four, beginning with the second British Open, in 1861 at Prestwick.

Young Tom dominated golf in Scotland in his short career, which ended with his tragic death in 1875 at the age of twenty-four.

In September, Young Tom and his father had traveled to North Berwick for a challenge match against Willie Park and his brother, Mungo. These matches were extremely popular and lucrative. Each player had wealthy financial backers. As much as hundreds of pounds could change hands, and the matches attracted large galleries.

The North Berwick match ended suddenly when word arrived that Young Tom's wife had become seriously ill following the birth of their child. Father and son raced for a ship waiting to take them across the Firth of Forth and home to St. Andrews.

Before the ship could sail, a second messenger arrived and told Old Tom the awful news: both mother and child had died.

Old Tom waited until St. Andrews was in view before telling his son, who was inconsolable.

Three months later, on Christmas morning, Young Tom died. Some say it was from drink. Others insist it was a broken heart.

Today, a plaque commemorating his life can be found at the ancient St. Andrews Cathedral. On it is written:

"Deeply regretted by numerous friends and all golfers, he thrice in succession won the championship belt and held it without rivalry and yet without envy, his many amiable qualities being no less acknowledged than his golfing achievements."

MOTHER ENGLAND

An older American couple was on a golf holiday through Scotland when they stopped in a small town near Balmoral, the Queen's country estate. As they wandered through the small shops, they spotted a distinguished woman, dressed in tweeds, who was looking at some of the goods. After a few moments, the American woman approached the lady.

"I must tell you that you look exactly like the Queen," the American said.

"How terribly reassuring," said the Queen, extending her hand.

Great Britain may have been under siege by the Nazis during World War II, but it didn't stop the Brits from playing golf—with a few modifications. Witness these "Temporary Rules, 1941, of the Richmond Golf Club, London."

1. Players are asked to collect the bomb and shrapnel splinters to save these from causing damage to the mowing machines.

2. In competitions, during gunfire or while bombs are falling, players may take shelter without penalty or ceasing play.
3. The positions of known delayed action bombs are marked by red flags at a reasonable, but not guaranteed, safe distance therefrom.
4. Shrapnel and/or bomb splinters on the Fairways, or in Bunkers, within a club's length of a ball, may be moved without penalty, and no penalty shall be incurred if a ball is thereby caused to move accidentally.
5. A ball moved by enemy action may be replaced, or if lost, or destroyed, a ball may be dropped not nearer the hole without penalty.
6. A ball lying in a crater may be lifted and dropped not nearer the hole, preserving the line to the hole, without penalty.
7. A player whose stroke is affected by the simultaneous explosion of a bomb may play another ball. Penalty: one stroke.

Henry Cotton was one of England's greatest golfers. He won three British Opens—an accomplishment that served only to fuel his considerable ego.

After finishing a round in the British Open one year, he was approached by a gentleman dressed in clothes that were more than a little on the garish side.

"Henry, great playing, pal," said the man as he enthusiastically pumped Cotton's hand.

"Thank you," said Cotton, his voice dripping with sarcasm. "And you must be an American."

Britain's Alison Nichols was a member of Europe's 1996 Solheim Cup team, which lost to the Americans in Wales. The key day for the Americans was Sunday, when they routed the Europeans, 10 to 2, in the singles play.

On Sunday morning, Nichols attended service at a small church near the golf course. At the service, she read from 1 Corinthians 9, verses 24–25, which reads, in part: "Know they not that they which run in a race run all, but one receiveth the prize? So run that ye may obtain."

In his newspaper column the following day, golf writer David Davies quoted Nichols, then wryly observed that "races, inevitably, go to the swift and yesterday the Americans were much the faster."

TOMMY NAKAJIMA

Like parents everywhere, Tommy Nakajima's father wanted to do everything he could to help his son develop his obvious talent for golf. And like parents everywhere, he realized that golf, like life, is no day at the beach.

So to help young Tommy prepare for rainy days, he built an enormous outdoor shower so Tommy could practice hitting balls in the rain.

And to help Tommy learn to play in the wind, he also set up a huge fan.

And since not every lie is a level lie, he came up with a practice tee that could be adjusted so Tommy would learn to play from all kinds of awkward stances.

And finally, since he knew tournament golf was a game of strength and stamina, he came up with a unique workout for Tommy: he had him run through the hills pulling a tire tied to his waist.

It's funny, but nothing ever seems to bother Tommy Nakajima on the golf course.

BYRON NELSON

Byron Nelson will always be ranked as one of the game's greatest champions, not only for the quality of his play but for the way he conducted himself both on and off the course. But what many people don't realize is that Nelson has a very dry sense of humor and—as his close friend Tom Watson once observed—a "bit of the ham in him." That sense of humor and timing was displayed at a PGA Tour dinner where he presented Greg Norman with the Tour's 1995 Byron Nelson Award.

"Byron, I'm just sorry we never had a chance to compete against each other," Norman said in his acceptance speech.

"I'm not," Byron replied quickly.

A few years after the death of his first wife, Louise, Byron remarried. His wife, Peggy, is a writer, and the two are totally devoted to one another. In 1995, fifty years after he won eleven tournaments in a row on tour, a writer asked Byron if he could play just one last round of golf with any

111

three players, who would the players be. The first person he named was Peggy.

"One day I was working on a piece of furniture in my workshop when the phone rang," Byron remembers. "I picked it up at the same time Peggy answered it in the house, but I didn't say anything. The caller was from an advertising agency in Dallas that wanted to pay me $25,000 to do an ad for a whiskey—Old Grand Dad, I think. Well, Peggy said to the man, 'You must not know Byron very well. He's never taken a drink in his life, and he'd never endorse something he doesn't believe in.' She thanked him for his interest, and that was that. A couple minutes later, she came out to the workshop.

"'Well, I see you cost me $25,000,' I joked."

Byron Nelson effectively retired from competitive golf in 1946, but he still played the occasional tournament. He played in the 1951 Bing Crosby Invitational as a favor to Bing, and won. In 1955, he and his wife, Louise, went to Europe with their good friends, the Eddie Lowerys—ostensibly for a vacation. Lowery, who had caddied for Francis Ouimet when Ouimet won the 1913 U.S. Open, convinced Byron to play in the British Open and then talked him into entering the French Open.

"Louise wasn't all too happy about me playing in the French Open since we were supposed to be on vacation, but when I saw the name of the street where we were staying I thought it might be a good omen.

The street was named "Rue Byron," and it was a good omen, indeed. Byron won the tournament.

JACK NICKLAUS

Sometimes inspiration comes where you least expect it. Just ask Jack Nicklaus.

Prior to the first round of the 1986 Masters, Tom McCollister, then a golf writer for the *Atlanta Journal-Constitution*, wrote a column handicapping the field at that year's tournament. When he got to Jack Nicklaus, he wrote the forty-six-year-old off as—among other things—"rusty," "done," and "washed up."

John Montgomery, a friend and business associate of Nicklaus, saw the column and taped it to the refrigerator of the house they were sharing in Augusta. While Nicklaus never mentioned the column, Montgomery knew he had seen it and that it had gotten his attention. In fact, it had angered him.

After shooting a final-round 65, Nicklaus was in the interview room while McCollister was in the main pressroom writing his story for the early editions. Nicklaus scanned the interview room looking for McCollister. He asked where the writer was, and Edwin Pope, a columnist for the Miami *Herald*, went to find him.

"Jack's looking for you," he told McCollister.

At the time, Nicklaus was explaining to the other writers how motivational the column had been. Just then, McCollister entered the room.

"Thank you, Tom," Nicklaus said, smiling.

"I'm just glad I could help," McCollister replied, as the room exploded in laughter.

Earlier in the day, on the par-3 16th hole, Nicklaus impressed his son, Jack Jr., with just how much experience counts at Augusta. After making an eagle on 15, Nicklaus hit a 5-iron on 16.

"Be the right club," said Jackie as the ball rose against the sky.

"It is," his father said, winking—even though his eyesight was so bad he couldn't see the ball land.

Maybe it was fate, but Nicklaus's Masters win in 1986 came in a year when his mother, Helen, decided to come to the tournament for only the second time. She had first come in 1959, when Nicklaus was first invited as an amateur. After her husband, Charlie, died in 1970, she never really felt up to making the trip. But in 1986, she told Jack she wanted to come back to Augusta one last time.

"It was her dream to see Jack win there one more time," explained her daughter-in-law, Barbara.

Even as an amateur, Jack Nicklaus's talents were undeniable. Tom Weiskopf has always said that when he first met Jack at Ohio State, Nicklaus was "already the best golfer in the world."

Nicklaus was paired with Don January in his first year at the Masters, 1959. On the 465-yard, par-5 13th hole, January outdrove Nicklaus by forty yards. He assumed that Nicklaus would lay up short of Rae's Creek. So did Nicklaus's caddie, Willie Peterson.

"Lay up, son," said Peterson. "You can't get there today."

Nicklaus blistered a 3-wood, which easily carried the creek and left him with an eagle putt.

"That kid's gonna run us all off the Tour," January said to his caddie.

Jack Nicklaus is one of those public figures who have a keen sense of how their comments are going to look in print the next day. As a result, he's usually pretty politic in his criticisms. But not always. After playing his first round at the 1970 U.S. Open at Hazeltine, the writers asked him what he thought about the controversial course.

"Excuse me while I go throw up," he said.

In the 1970s, Jack Nicklaus developed an interest in wine and set out to learn all he could about the subject. One night at a PGA Tour dinner his knowledge was tested by veteran writer Dick Taylor, a longtime friend.

The evening's wine selections were brought to the Nicklaus-Taylor table wrapped in linen.

"All right, Jack, let's see how much you really know," Taylor said. "Let's see if you can identify what these wines are."

Nicklaus went through the elaborate ritual of swirling the wine in the glass, breathing the wine's bouquet, and tasting it. He puzzled over the wines momentarily, then identified them perfectly.

"I was astonished," Taylor recalls. "The next day I ran into [then–PGA Tour commissioner] Deane Beman and told him how impressed I was that Jack was so knowledgeable about the wine."

"Well, he should have been, Dick," Beman said, laughing. "I asked him to pick out the wine for last night's dinner."

The Nicklaus household has always been crawling with kids: their five children, their children's friends, and now their growing number of grandchildren.

One evening Jack returned home after winning a senior tour event. He pointed out that he won with six new clubs in his bag.

"Were they all woods?" asked one of his son Gary's friends.

Fourteen-year-old Jack Nicklaus arrived for a practice round at the 1954 Ohio Amateur. Pouring rains kept most of the competitors inside, but Nicklaus was drawn to the steady crack of balls being hit by a solitary figure on the practice range. The man was hitting a short iron, but the ball tore off the clubface like it was a 1-iron. Nicklaus was impressed. So impressed, in fact, that he asked who the player was.

"Arnold Palmer," he was told. It was the beginning of a long rivalry. The rest of the rivalry was, as they say, history.

It's probably inevitable, but when Tiger Woods emerged as the finest amateur of the current era, people began comparing him to Jack Nicklaus. Tom Weiskopf, who has known Nicklaus since their days together at Ohio State, put it all into perspective—from his unique perspective.

"When Jack was at Ohio State, he was already the best player in the world. Period. And this was at a time when Arnold was winning most of his Majors and Hogan and Snead were still playing. That's how good Jack was."

And if Nicklaus's play in the 1960 U.S. Open at Cherry Hills is any indication, Weiskopf might well be right. As a twenty-year-old amateur, Nicklaus finished second to Arnold Palmer.

Nicklaus was paired with Ben Hogan in the final round, and Hogan summed up Nicklaus's play this way:

"I just played with a kid who should have won the Open by ten shots," Hogan told the writers.

GREG NORMAN

Following his devastating loss in the 1996 Masters, Greg Norman decided to take a break from golf. He, Nick Price, their wives, and a few other friends boarded Norman's yacht, *Aussie Rules*, and cruised south. After a few days of fishing and relaxing, they discovered a nine-hole course on Cat Cay. Norman, his brother-in-law, and two crew members headed for the course. Days later, somebody asked Greg if he liked the course.

"It's hard to say," Norman said. "We had eighteen beers for eighteen holes. When the beer ran out, we quit."

MOE NORMAN

Over the years, Canada's Moe Norman has become something of a cult figure—albeit an unlikely one. Norman was self-taught, played fast, said everything twice, and was generally regarded as one of the finest ballstrikers in golf history. He rarely left Canada, and when he did he traveled by bus, not quite trusting in the miracle of flight.

On one of his rare visits to America, he was playing in a tournament. Because of nerves or whatever reason, he was playing even faster than normal—normal being a virtual breakneck speed compared with the other pros. Finally, one of his playing partners tried to get him to slow down.

"Moe, just relax and take your time," the pro said.

"Why?" Moe answered. "The greens aren't moving. The greens aren't moving."

The late George Knudson, a fellow Canadian, enjoyed a successful career on the PGA Tour. He was a great student and admirer of Ben Hogan as well as one of the first players to acknowledge Moe Norman's considerable skills. At a dinner honoring Norman, he compared the two men.

"I believe that the only other player to ever rank with Moe as a ballstriker was Ben Hogan," Knudson said. "Nobody else was even close."

Moe Norman broke into tears and covered his face with his hands.

PORKY OLIVER

Ed "Porky" Oliver won four times on the Tour, but after one of his wins, he didn't have much to show for it.

As he was on his way out of the clubhouse following the awards ceremony, he ran into a card game and was persuaded to join in for a few hands. It was a particularly friendly game, and a few hands turned into a few hours. When it was all over, Porky had not lost only all his tournament winnings, but the car he'd won as well.

Did it bother him?

Not particularly. He wandered into the parking lot and hitched a ride with some friends to the next tournament.

FRANCIS OUIMET

Francis Ouimet's win in the 1913 U.S. Open was easily one of the great upsets in all of sports. Ouimet was a twenty-year-old amateur facing the two great British professionals, Harry Vardon and Ted Ray, in a playoff at The Country Club in Brookline, Massachusetts—the course where Ouimet had learned the game as a caddie. To say that there wasn't a lot of conversation between the players that day is an understatement.

"When they congratulated me on the 18th green, it was the first time either had spoken to me all day," he recalled. "They didn't talk to me, and I was afraid to speak to them."

Ouimet was an enormously popular and respected figure in Great Britain. He was the first American to be named Captain of the Royal and Ancient Golf Club of St. Andrews and served as a model for generations of players, both professional and amateur.

When Ouimet died on September 22, 1967, his obituary ran for 1½ columns on the front page of *The Times* of London—a remarkable tribute to a remarkable man.

ARNOLD PALMER

Throughout his career, Arnold Palmer has given the galleries at the Masters plenty of reasons to cheer—although one year he got an ovation that left him shaking his head.

"I was leading the tournament on Sunday and the galleries were pretty big, even for Augusta. I hit my drive on 11, and I walked off the tee and went into the woods on the left to relieve myself. When I walked out of the trees the gallery gave me this great ovation. It was pretty embarrassing, to be honest with you."

At the 1995 Masters, a plaque honoring Arnold Palmer was unveiled at Augusta National. The plaque, which is about thirty inches tall and two feet wide, is attached to a water fountain near the tee on the par-3 16th hole.

During his second round that year, Palmer approached the large gallery near the tee and asked if the water was any good.

"It's holy water, Arnie," one of his fans replied.

Palmer laughed along with the gallery, then went ahead and birdied the hole. As he left the green, he said, "If they'd put a plaque up for me on every hole, I could really play this course."

Arnold Palmer has a phenomenal record at Augusta, winning in 1958, 1960, 1962, and 1964 and finishing second in 1961 and 1965. In fact, in 1961 he came very close to becoming the first player to win back-to-back Masters.

With Gary Player sitting in a cottage watching Palmer on television, Arnold came to the 18th hole with a one-stroke lead. After hitting a good drive, he approached his ball in the fairway. A friend, George Low, congratulated him on winning the tournament. Palmer thanked him and thought to himself, "Well, that's it. Just get the ball on the green somewhere and make a 4." It was just enough to take his focus off playing the shot.

He hit a 7-iron into the right bunker and the ball buried slightly. Instead of playing a safe shot, Palmer tried to get the ball close. Instead, he hit it thin and sent the ball over the green and down a slope into the gallery. He hit a poor chip and left himself a twenty-footer for a tie. He missed.

"I was in shock," Palmer admitted. "I always thought 6s happened to the other guy."

There's a theory that holds that almost every golfer at some point suffers a loss so devastating that it effectively ends his or her career. Tom Weiskopf admits that, for him, it was losing to Jack Nicklaus in the 1975 Masters—his fourth and last second-place finish at Augusta.

People close to Ben Hogan say his game was never quite the same after he finished second to Dr. Cary Middlecoff at the 1956 U.S. Open at Oak Hill.

And people who follow the game believe that Arnold Palmer never recovered from blowing a seven-stroke lead with nine holes left to play at the 1966 U.S. Open at San Francisco's Olympic Club.

"It looks like second is the best I can do," said Palmer's playing companion, Billy Casper, as he made the turn on Sunday.

"I'll do everything I can do to help you," Palmer replied graciously.

He did more than anyone dreamed possible.

Hoping to set an Open record, Palmer attacked the back nine. He gave up a shot at 10 and another at 13. He gave back two more on 15 and two on 16. He lost another on 17 and barely managed to par 18 to force a Monday playoff, which he lost, 69–73.

"I've never seen anything like it," Casper said later. "I tried to talk to him after we putted out on Sunday, but he was in shock. Total shock. I've never seen anything like it."

There's never been a golfer—or possibly any public figure—who has enjoyed a better relationship with the press than Arnold Palmer. He's always been fair and open to the writers, and they have responded in kind.

One year at Augusta, Palmer was in contention going into the final round and played horribly, shooting an 81 that included a missed four-inch putt.

Palmer went to the locker room following his round and was sitting dejectedly by his locker, sipping a beer, when a group of writers quietly approached.

"Arnold, we hate to bother you at a time like this . . ." said one of his friends.

Palmer looked up and smiled.

"Boys, we've talked when the times were good, and we'll talk when the times are bad," he said.

HARVEY PENICK

Among the thousands of people who sought out Harvey Penick for lessons, one was Betsy Rawls. She first came to Mr. Penick as a student at the University of Texas, and the woman who would go on to win four U.S. Women's Opens was immediately impressed.

"Harvey changed my grip slightly and then charged me $3 for my first lesson," she says. "When I finished my second lesson, I asked how much I owed him. 'Nothing. I'm just telling you the same thing I told you the other day.' And he was absolutely serious. He wouldn't take a cent."

One morning Tom Kite brought a friend—a writer—to Austin Country Club for a round of golf. Tom's father joined them, and when they made the turn Harvey Penick arrived at the tee in his golf cart. Penick followed them for three holes. This must have inspired the writer, who made two birdies and a par.

"What do you think, Mr. Penick?" Tom asked. "Does he have any talent?"

"Your friend has all the talent in the world," Penick replied softly. "The question is, 'Does he believe?'"

Of all the great players Harvey Penick touched, he was especially close to Ben Crenshaw and Tom Kite. While Tom moved to Austin, Texas, as a twelve-year-old, Mr. Penick had known Ben since he was a youngster.

"My dad arranged for me to take lessons from Harvey beginning when I was about seven," remembers Crenshaw. "The first thing he did was put my hands on the club, which was an old mashie he found back in the storeroom and cut down for me. He never told me how I should hold it. He just very gently placed my hands on the club. After he was satisfied with my grip, he gave me a little putter and a ball and told me to chip the ball onto the practice green and then putt it into the hole. I think I said something like, 'Gosh, Mr. Penick, I want to play golf,' and he said, 'Ben, you are playing golf.'"

In the spring of 1995, Harvey Penick was near death. Both Kite and Crenshaw made special efforts to visit their old friend and teacher. On one visit—near the end—Penick asked Ben how he was playing. Crenshaw told him that, of all things, he wasn't putting very well. Penick asked Ben to get a putter and hit a few putts.

"Ben, I want you to trust yourself," he said weakly. "Just make two good practice strokes and then hit it—and don't let the putterhead pass your hands."

A few days later, Harvey Penick died. And a few days after that, Ben Crenshaw won his second Masters.

"Harvey always told us to 'take dead aim,' and that's been widely quoted," says Crenshaw. "I've often wondered if people really understand what he meant. He wanted you to trust yourself and not think about anything else but the shot at hand. Let your instincts take over and believe with all your heart that you can hit the shot you want to hit."

After Penick's funeral—where Crenshaw and Kite served as pallbearers—Crenshaw was talking with his brother, Charlie. He said something his brother had never heard him say before.

"I wished him good luck and he said, 'Charlie, I just feel I can win it. If I can just get off to a good start, I know I'll be all right,'" Charlie said. "It stuck in my mind, because it was so unlike Ben. He just had this sense that it was meant to be."

A writer asked Ben if it was different winning the Masters for the second time.

"I got a lot more mail than ever before," said Crenshaw. "Somebody sent me a pair of underwear and asked me to autograph them. I wrote back and thanked them for their interest, and I didn't want to seem rude, but there was a limit to what I'd sign."

PINE VALLEY GOLF CLUB

Any listing of America's best golf courses invariably finds Pine Valley at or near the top, and with good reason: it is beautiful, demanding, surprisingly fair, and as visually intimidating as any course in the world.

So it was with considerable intimidation that Fred Raphael—the producer and director of the old "Shell's Wonderful World of Golf"—accepted an invitation to play his very first round of golf—ever—at Pine Valley, where the inaugural match would be played between Byron Nelson and Gene Littler.

"My old friend Gene Sarazen got a set of clubs for me from Wilson, and when he found out where I was playing he gave me six dozen of the smaller British golf balls," Raphael recalls. "I was playing with some members who worked for Shell. I think I shot about 150. About a month later, all the members got a letter from the club's president, Mr. John Arthur Brown, announcing that some twenty-nine illegal British balls had been found on the property, and if Mr. J. Arthur Brown found out who was using illegal balls, he would personally toss them out of the club. My friend from Shell asked me what I thought we should do. I told him to write Mr. Brown and tell him to keep looking. There were four more balls out there somewhere."

GARY PLAYER

Over the years, Gary Player has been fanatical about his health and fitness, but on at least one occasion being in good shape paid off for the great South African champion.

Player was driving to the golf course for the second round in the 1974 Masters. As usual, traffic was backed up along Washington Road, and Player began to nervously check the time for fear he'd be late. Then, to make matters worse, his car got a flat tire. Player pulled off the road, jumped out of the car, and ran to the golf course—about a mile away.

Two days later, he left his house for the final round, only to find that his car wouldn't start. Player hitchhiked to the course and went on to win his second of three Green Jackets.

Masters champions are allowed to keep their Green Jacket with them for a year after their win. After that, the jackets are returned to Augusta National. Gary Player is the only exception. After winning in 1974, he neglected to bring the jacket with him the following year.

"I always assumed that if they wanted it back that badly they'd travel to South Africa and get it," he explained.

One day Gary Player was approached by a young man who asked for his autograph. Player happily signed, but then gave the teenager a bit of advice.

"Young man, I'm going to tell you something and you must pay attention to what I'm saying: You must lose some weight. You're terribly overweight. Your parents won't tell you this because they love you and don't want to hurt your feelings. I don't want to hurt your feelings either, but you must lose those pounds."

With that, he shook the stunned kid's hand, gave him the autograph, and walked away.

POLITICIANS

While many of his critics have criticized Bill Clinton for some of his fundraising tactics, there was at least one occasion when no one could argue that it went to a good cause.

When his daughter, Chelsea, was a student at the Sidwell Friends School, in Washington, Clinton agreed to take part in an auction to raise money for the school. The prize was a round of golf with the President. The bidding was spirited, and the winner was a civil servant who, by all accounts, must have been a big Bill Clinton fan.

He won the round with a bid of $76,000.

With any luck, the President threw in a sleeve of autographed golf balls.

When Dan Quayle was running for vice president in 1988, his opponents dragged up a bogus story by a woman claiming that she'd had a relationship with Quayle during a Florida golf vacation he'd taken with some other congressmen—a trip that lasted all of one day. The press ran with the story for a while, until Quayle's wife, Marilyn—who has a wonderfully dry sense of humor—deftly killed it.

"Anyone who knows Dan knows that given the choice between golf and sex, he'll choose golf every time," she quipped. And the story vaporized overnight.

At the time the story was playing out in the papers, a writer asked Tip O'Neill what he thought. Tip, who shared a warm friendship with Quayle that was based in no small part on their mutual love of golf, dismissed it. Then he noted, for good measure, that "when a fella gets to be my age, the biggest thrill you can look forward to is running in a long putt."

Richard Nixon was a determined—if ungainly—golfer. One evening, when he was vice president, he spoke at a golf writers' dinner in New York City. He began by pointing out that while he wasn't much of a golfer, he had beaten a girl named Barbara in a match played a few weeks earlier.

It turned out the girl was Barbara McIntire, the reigning U.S. Women's Amateur champion.

It turned out that she had played from the men's tees.

And it turned out that she had given the vice president fourteen strokes.

Other than that, it was quite an accomplishment.

William Howard Taft may not have been America's greatest president, but weighing in at some 300 pounds, he was easily one of the largest. In spite of his bulk, he was a passionate golfer and not altogether bad, either.

One of his friends was Herbert Leeds, who designed the Myopia Hunt Club in the suburbs of Boston and ran the place like a despot. Myopia can be a brutally difficult course, in no small measure because of the deep pot bunkers that dot the course.

One afternoon in 1910, Taft visited Myopia for a match with Leeds. Taft wasn't exactly on his game—such as his game was—and routinely found himself having to escape from the bunkers.

Finally, on the 10th hole, he encountered a bunker that was too deep for him to get out of. Literally. After hitting his ball out of the bunker he tried to crawl out, but found after several tries that he couldn't. Finally, a caddie was sent back to the clubhouse for some strong rope, which was tied around Taft's considerable waist so he could be pulled from the bunker. To his credit, though, the game continued.

Nothing bothered Mr. Leeds more than seeing a player shoot a low score on his beloved course. He was notorious for ordering bunkers placed in a spot where he saw a player hit an especially good drive. In the years following his death, no small amount of time and money was spent filling in some of his more excessive bunkering.

At any rate, one day in 1926 British golfer George Sargent arrived at Myopia for a day of golf. With him was Linde

Fowler, a golf writer for the now-defunct *Boston Transcript*. Sargent shot a 69 in the morning. The thought that a player could break 70 the first time he saw Myopia was too much for Mr. Leeds. During Sargent's lunch break, he ordered all the pins tucked in difficult spots and had the tee markers moved as far back as possible.

It worked. Sort of.

In the afternoon round Sargent skied to a 1-under 71. As he and Fowler walked off the final green, Leeds approached them. Instead of congratulating Sargent for his outstanding play, he ordered Fowler not to write a word about Sargent's play in the *Transcript* . . . and he didn't.

THE PRESS

Bernard Darwin, who wrote for *The Times* of London, was probably the first powerful golf writer—or at least the first golf writer the players actually paid any attention to.

Following one of his rounds in a tournament, the six-time British Open champion Harry Vardon was congratulated on his play.

"Thank you, but merely shooting a good score is insufficient," said Vardon. "I never really know how well I've played until I read Mr. Darwin's verdict in *The Times*."

Dick Taylor, who was the editor of *Golf World* for more decades than he'd care to remember, is one of the game's most astute observers. Over the years he's seen virtually every player and tournament worth seeing. On more than one occasion a player has felt the sting of his considerable wit. And sometimes he got as good as he gave.

He was at Congressional watching Jack Nicklaus play a practice round prior to the 1995 U.S. Senior Open. Nicklaus, an old friend, walked over to the ropes to say hello to Taylor.

After a few moments, Nicklaus started to walk away. But before he left he told Taylor, "If you're looking for your friend [1913 U.S. Open champion] Francis Ouimet, he's two holes ahead of us."

Peter Dobereiner, who died in 1996 at the age of seventy, was said to be the most widely read golf writer in the world, and there is no reason to doubt that. Dobers, as he was known, had been the golf correspondent for England's *Daily Mail*, *The Guardian,* and *The Observer,* and a contributing editor and columnist for *Golf Digest*.

One of his friends was Renton Laidlaw, a Scotsman who reported on golf tournaments around the world for the British Broadcasting Corporation. Laidlaw would phone his reports from the pressroom, and to help silence the din, he would occasionally put a box over his head.

One day he was seated near Dobers, and in the course of his broadcast he reported that play had been postponed by rain. With that, Dobers went into action. He walked over and began tapping gently on the top of the box.

"Ah," said Laidlaw. "I think you can hear the rain coming down now."

Peter Dobereiner knew the ability of a well-aimed and slyly delivered barb to deflate even the largest and healthiest of egos. Take Jack Nicklaus, for example.

One evening Peter and some other writers were invited to join Jack at a dinner in St. Andrews. The waiter grandly announced that one of the evening's entrées would be a magnificent salmon caught that day by none other than that noted angler, Jack William Nicklaus, himself.

"It's just my luck," Dobereiner said, loud enough for Nicklaus to overhear. "I'll probably get the piece that contains the bullet."

Nicklaus took the bait—so to speak—and insisted that Dobereiner sit next to him at dinner.

For decades now, the Golf Writers Association of America has held a tournament in Myrtle Beach, South Carolina, on the weekend prior to the Masters. In 1965, they invited the executive secretary of the United States Golf Association, Joseph C. Dey, to compete in the tournament.

Dey, who began his career covering golf for a Philadelphia newspaper, accepted. Everything was fine until he attended a pretournament cocktail party that featured an auction of the field. This put Dey—a man of great rectitude—in an awkward position. The USGA had taken a strong stand against such auctions on the heels of a scandal surrounding a Calcutta at the Deepdale Country Club Invitational in the 1950s.

When Bob Drum, the association's president, began auctioning off teams, Dey voiced his concerns.

"Bob, this isn't a Calcutta, is it?" he asked.

"Nope, it's a Bombay," the Drummer replied.

Almost to a person, writers are great procrastinators. If we can find a way to put off writing a piece, we'll do it. Any excuse will do. None is too trivial. For some reason, this is especially true when it comes to books. Maybe the sheer volume of the work required is simply too daunting. Whatever the reason, it usually takes the magical combination of a deadline and a dwindling bank balance to produce the required inspiration.

That was certainly the case with the legendary Herb Graffis. In a business filled with colorful characters, Herb Graffis stepped—full-blown—from the "Front Page."

"I was doing a book with Sam Snead and we'd already blown the deadline," Graffis once explained. "The publishers were screaming about money and contracts and all that usual publisher's stuff, so I went down to the 1938 PGA Championship at Shawnee-on-Delaware. I talked to Sam a little bit, and then I went back to my room at the hotel. It was miserably hot and humid and there was no air-conditioning, so I did the only sane thing: I took off all my clothes, wrapped a towel around my waist, and sat down at the typewriter with a case of cold beer. When I woke up the next morning, the beer was gone and the book was done."

Herb Graffis once gave a young writer a valuable piece of advice.

"Son," he said. "Well-meaning people are always going to tell you to 'write what you know.' That's nonsense. Do that and you'll starve. In this business, you've got to write what they'll pay you to write."

B ob Harlow was a golf promoter and writer who started *Golf World* magazine in 1947. And while he loved golf he was even fonder of good food, and fancied himself as something of a gourmet. Occasionally he got carried away with his fascination with food. In fact, one year the first eight pages of copy he filed from the U.S. Open were devoted to his visits to the area's best restaurants—which means that, in the glorious tradition of golf writers everywhere, he didn't exactly race to pick up a check that week.

CHI CHI RODRIGUEZ

Chi Chi Rodriguez grew up in Puerto Rico, and if his family wasn't poor, they were close enough to poverty to see what it looked like.

It's not surprising, then, that when he grew old enough to caddie, he jumped at the chance to earn some money for himself. Of course, it helped that he was fascinated by the game.

He was tremendously devoted to his father, who would sit with each of his children for fifteen minutes every evening when he came home from work. One night he was sitting with Chi Chi and he asked him how his school day had been. Chi Chi told him it had been great.

"Then he looked down at my shoes and saw grass clippings stuck to the sides," Chi Chi remembered. "He told me, 'Son, they don't have grass growing in the classrooms.' When he asked me where I'd been, I admitted I'd skipped school and gone to the golf course to caddie. He told me to give him the money I'd earned. It taught me two lessons: first, don't lie, and second, share what I had with others. They were two of the most important lessons I ever learned."

BOB ROSBURG

M ost people today know Bob Rosburg as a commentator
for ABC's golf coverage, but he was an outstanding
player. He won the 1959 PGA Championship and he came
close to winning a couple of U.S. Opens. Along the way, he
developed a knack for walking off the course if the mood
struck him.

Dave Marr remembered that when he sent Rossie and his
wife, Eleanor, a note when they celebrated their 18th wed-
ding anniversary: "Eleanor, congratulations on performing a
miracle. Rossie rarely goes all 18."

THE ROYAL AND ANCIENT GOLF CLUB OF ST. ANDREWS

The Old Course at St. Andrews has seen more golf history than any other course in the world. In fact, here's a good trivia question. Every great player in history has walked across the old stone bridge on the 18th hole at St. Andrews. Except one: Ben Hogan.

Hogan played in just one British Open—1953, at Carnoustie. He never visited St. Andrews, let alone played the Old Course.

Ben Sayers, a legendary Scottish player, professional, and club maker, traveled to the United States in 1914 to visit his son, George, then the professional at Merion. When he arrived in the States, he sent a postcard to his great friend and rival, Andrew Kirkaldy, of St. Andrews. The card was addressed simply:

Andra.
Hell Bunker.
St. Andrews, Scotland.

150

THE RULES

Bill Campbell is one of America's greatest amateurs. As a former president of the United States Golf Association and a captain of the R & A, he's a person you'd certainly expect to know the rules of golf inside and out. Still, even someone like Bill Campbell can occasionally run afoul of the rules—as he did during the 1946 NCAA championship at Springdale Golf Club in New Jersey.

Campbell was playing for Princeton and had to be considered one of the tournament favorites. He started on the back nine this day, and when he came to the 18th hole he hit his drive into a pond. After studying his options, he elected to play his third shot from the women's tee. All perfectly legal. But the trouble came when he teed up the ball. This would have been allowable if he'd gone back to tournament markers, but the rules forbid him from teeing the ball on the women's tee.

At any rate, Campbell drove the green and sank a long putt for what he assumed was a remarkable par. As he walked off the green he ran into Howie Stepp, the coach of the Princeton swim team, who was serving as a rules official at the championship.

"That was some shot, Bill," Stepp said. "What did you hit?"

"A driver, coach," Campbell answered.

"A driver? Off the turf?" Stepp asked.

Campbell realized his mistake.

"Bill, we're going to make a new rule just for you—two strokes for stupidity," Stepp joked.

In the heat of competition, it's sometimes easy to overlook a rule—sometimes with painful consequences. Take the case of Lloyd Mangrum.

Mangrum tied with Ben Hogan and George Fazio at the end of seventy-two holes in the 1950 U.S. Open at Merion. As he stood over his putt on the 16th hole in the playoff, he noticed a bug resting on his ball. Not thinking, he marked the ball with his putter, picked up the ball, and blew the bug off.

Big mistake. He was penalized two strokes and wound up shooting a 73. Hogan won the playoff with a 69.

Joe Dey, the highly respected executive director of the United States Golf Association, was the rules official with amateur Billy Joe Patton when Patton made his run at the 1954 Masters.

Patton led by a stroke after thirty-six holes, but a third-round 75 left him trailing Ben Hogan and Sam Snead. In the final round, he was cruising along making pars until he came to the 6th hole, a downhill par 3. He hit a 5-iron and watched as the ball trickled into the cup, wedging itself between the flagstick and the side of the cup. The enormous roar from the gallery attracted people following Hogan on the nearby 3rd hole, and they raced over to see what had happened.

As Patton and Dey reached the green, Dey walked over to the hole and cautioned Patton to carefully move the flag, for fear that the ball might pop out of the cup. When Patton nudged the stick, the ball dropped to the bottom of the cup and he had his ace.

Patton went on to birdie the 8th and 9th holes to tie for the lead, but gambles on the 13th and 15th cost him a shot at a playoff with Snead and Hogan the following day. Still, it wasn't a complete loss. A week later, he was invited back to Augusta for a round with President Dwight D. Eisenhower.

Sam Snead was as fierce a competitor as ever played the game. As much as he loved winning, he hated losing even more. And he was always figuring the odds. To make sure he never played the wrong ball, he had Wilson make his Staff balls with a "0." Sam was the only player they ever did that for.

Still, occasionally he did slip up. In 1960, he was playing Mason Rudolph in a made-for-television match at Bermuda's Mid-Ocean Club. It was a great match, and they came to the final hole all even. As he stood on the tee, Sam noticed that he had fifteen clubs in his bag. He didn't know what to do. If he told Rudolph and the officials, he was afraid he'd ruin the show. Cheating—and not telling anyone—was out of the question, so he finished the match by three-putting the final green—allowing Rudolph to win.

He thought that would be the end of it, but a few days later a story broke in the New York *Mirror* charging that Sam had tanked the match. The PGA of America reviewed the charges, and ruled that Sam had done nothing wrong. Still, the story bothered Sam for years afterward.

Ever hear of Burt Whittmore? Probably not, but if it weren't for a brush with the rules, he might well have won the 1898 U.S. Open at the Myopia Hunt Club near Boston.

He was in contention in the final round when he came to the 12th hole, a brutally difficult par 4. The hole was cut in the back of the severely sloping green. Whittmore's ball was on the front of the green. He hit the ball firmly, then watched in horror as it slid off the green and down a bank into the deep rough.

Things got worse very soon after that.

He and his caddie searched for the ball. So did his fellow players and their caddies. The gallery helped out, but to no avail. Burt Whittmore became the first and no doubt only player ever to lose an Open by losing a ball on a putt. In fact, he may be the only player *ever* to lose a ball on a putt.

And then there's the story of Denis Watson. At the time of the 1985 U.S. Open, Watson was one of the best players in the game. He had won three PGA Tour events the previous year and came within a rules misunderstanding of winning the '85 Open at Oakland Hills.

Playing the 8th hole in the first round, he had a ten-foot par putt. The ball came to rest on the edge of the cup, literally on the verge of dropping into the hole. Watson waited. And waited. And waited some more—some thirty seconds in all. Finally, the ball dropped into the hole. Relieved, Watson headed for the next tee, only to be met by a rules official, Montford Johnson, who had some very bad news—three strokes' worth, in fact. One for the tap-in Watson should have made, and two for violating the rule concerning delay of play.

Watson finished the Open one stroke behind the winner, Andy North.

Until the early 1970s, simply saying you were thinking of turning pro was enough to cost you your amateur status. There's a story about the young man who wrote the United States Golf Association:

> "Dear Sirs—I think I'd like to become a professional. How do I do it?"

> "Dear Sir—You just did" was the USGA's reply.

GENE SARAZEN

One of the benefits of age is that it gives you a certain perspective on things. Take winning, for example. At the
1996 Masters, a writer asked ninety-four-year-old Gene
Sarazen what he thought about two-time U.S. Amateur
champion Tiger Woods.

"He's a good player," said Sarazen. "Of course, when I
was his age [twenty] I won the U.S. Open and the PGA
Championship."

Gene Sarazen, Sam Snead, and Byron Nelson are the official starters at the Masters, teeing off in the ceremonial
first group on Thursday mornings.

On the day before the start of the 1996 Masters, Sarazen
ran into Sam in the clubhouse. After a while, their conversation turned to the modern equipment, and Sam told him
that he had a new driver he was excited about.

"I guess that means you'll outdrive me tomorrow,"
Sarazen, then ninety-four, joked.

In 1932, after winning the U.S. and British Opens, Gene Sarazen was invited to speak at Colgate University. Despite his self-assurance, he was a man of limited formal education and the prospect of addressing a hall filled with college students was intimidating.

After he was introduced, he received a warm ovation and nervously approached the lectern.

"Thanks a lot, I'm happy to be here," he stammered before quickly taking his seat.

Fortunately, his friend, architect Robert Trent Jones, was in the audience. Jones rose and asked Sarazen to tell the students about a celebrated match he'd had with Walter Hagen.

Well, the result was magical. Sarazen got up and launched into his story, complete with imitations of Hagen. The students loved it, and Sarazen spoke for over an hour.

Later, he told Jones how much he enjoyed it.

"Those kids loved it," he said. "I think I'll do this at all the colleges."

A few years later, Trent Jones invited Sarazen and Sam Snead to come up and play an exhibition match at one of his new courses. He offered them $100 each. The exhibition was a huge success, and the following year he asked them back.

"Okay, we'll come, but last time we had to pay all our expenses ourselves," Sarazen explained. "We didn't make a cent. This time we'll do it for the gate."

Jones agreed, and at the end of the exhibition he gave them their payment—$98 each.

"Hey, what gives here, Trent?" Sam asked. "There were a lot more people out there this time."

"Yes, Sam, but there are no fences around the course," Trent replied. "Most of the people just snuck in."

In 1973, Gene Sarazen traveled to Royal Troon for the British Open, just as he had fifty years earlier. At the time of his first visit he was a heavy favorite to win the championship, and with good reason. As a mere twenty-year-old he had won the 1922 U.S. Open and PGA Championship and was already being compared favorably to two of his great friends and rivals, Bob Jones and Walter Hagen.

For all the hype and anticipation, though, his first trip to Troon was a failure. He failed to qualify due to torrential rains and left for America, vowing to return—"even if I have to swim all the way across the Atlantic."

In the years that followed he would play competitively in six British Opens, winning in 1932 at Prince's, Sandwich, and finishing second once, third twice, and never finishing out of the Top Ten.

But it was in 1973, through the power of television, that Sarazen, then seventy-one, captured the imagination of the golfing world. Playing the treacherous par-3 8th—the "Postage Stamp" hole—he holed a punched 5-iron for a hole-in-one. The gallery roared in celebration for the first of only four men to win the modern Grand Slam—the U.S. and British Opens, the Masters, and the PGA Championship.

"They brought me into the press tent for my interview, and when I was finished they brought in a German kid who had made a 13 on the hole," Sarazen remembered years later.

"They asked him how it could be that an old man like me could make an ace on a hole while he made a 13. The kid thought for a second and then said, 'I three-putted.'"

When Gene Sarazen became one of the hosts of "Shell's Wonderful World of Golf" in the 1960s and early '70s, he was introduced to a whole generation of people who had never seen him play. One of the most poignant moments in the long history of the series came when Sarazen sat down for a visit with Bob Jones. Jones was virtually crippled by this time, and it was a testimony to the two men's deep friendship that Jones agreed to the interview.

In the course of the interview, they marveled at the similarities in their lives.

They were born seven weeks apart. They were married—to women named Mary—one week apart. They both played in their first U.S. Open in 1920.

There was a pause in the conversation, then Jones looked at Sarazen and said: "We didn't do too bad, did we?"

Gene Sarazen was in his sixties when the "Liberty Mutual Legends of Golf" got its start, but he was delighted to be back in the spotlight. In one of the event's early years, he and Paul Runyan were played with Arnold Palmer and Dow Finsterwald in the first round. As the teams were announced to the huge gallery surrounding the first tee, Sarazen leaned over to the tournament founder, Fred Raphael, and whispered, "Who's your money on?"

Raphael laughed, but at the end of nine holes, the teams were all even.

It might not be fair to say that Sarazen was cocky, but it would certainly be accurate to say that he never lacked for confidence. Following his first U.S. Open win, in 1922 at Skokie Country Club, he told the writers: "All men are created free and equal—and I am one shot better than the rest."

SHOW BUSINESS

In 1952, Katherine Hepburn and Spencer Tracy filmed the classic movie *Pat and Mike*. The golf scenes were shot at Riviera Country Club in Los Angeles.

Hepburn, as it happened, was quite a good golfer in her own right. Early in the shooting, the scene called for her to hit a twenty-foot putt. She studied the line, set up over the ball, and drilled it into the heart of the cup on the first take. Naturally, she was thrilled.

"No, no, no," cried the director, George Cukor. "You're supposed to miss it. Do it again. And don't try so hard this time."

CHARLIE SIFFORD

One of the great benefits to the stunning success of Tiger
Woods is the reflected light that shines on minority golf-
ers who went before him—players like Ted Rhodes, Bill
Spiller, Lee Elder, and Charlie Sifford.

While many talented black golfers never had a chance to
play the Tour, Sifford did and carried himself with distinc-
tion. Like Elder, his struggle was heightened because he
played at a time when the civil rights movement was shap-
ing—and shaking—America, to the considerable resentment
of many. The racism was occasionally subtle; but more often
than not, people didn't bother with the subtleties.

In 1965, Sifford entered a tournament at the Pensacola
(Florida) Country Club. Prior to the first round, he walked
into the clubhouse dining room and ordered breakfast. He
was just about to begin eating his meal when a man
approached.

"Excuse me, Charlie, but you can't eat here," he said, nervously. "This is a private dining room. Please don't make any
trouble."

Charlie Sifford was mortified. But rather than cause a
scene, he quietly took his breakfast and went to the locker
room to eat. A few minutes later he was joined by Bob Rosburg, Ken Venturi, and Frank Stranahan, who ate with him—

sending a powerful signal to the members and tournament officials alike.

Charlie Sifford shot a 63 to lead after the first round of the 1955 Canadian Open. One of the top players at the time shot a 64, and the two were paired together the next day.

"Who's Charlie Sifford, and how'd he shoot a 63?" the player asked in the locker room.

"The same way you did," Sifford said, extending his hand. "One stroke at a time. I'm Charlie Sifford."

"Oh," the player said. "Well, it's nice to meet you, Charlie."

SAM SNEAD

Lee Trevino once called Sam Snead "America's greatest athlete," and people who saw him in his prime wouldn't be inclined to argue. He had strength, grace, and remarkable suppleness. He could bend over and take a ball out of the cup without bending his knees. He could extend his right arm, place a driver between his first two fingers, and hold the driver parallel to the ground. And then there was the business about the doorjambs.

"I vividly recall being in the locker room at Oakland Hills during the 1979 PGA Championship," says Gary Player. "Sam was doing very well that week, and the young players were just marveling at his play. I was telling several of them some stories about Sam when I saw him enter the locker room. I bet them that even at age sixty-seven, Sam could still kick the top of the doorjamb—which is eight feet from the floor. They took my bet and I called over to Sam, challenging him to see if he could still do it. Naturally, Sam never turned down a challenge like that, and to the young players' astonishment he did it quite easily. As I remember, Sam and I split the money, too."

Sam Snead may never have won the U.S. Open, but he was the leading money winner at the Open in 1937 when Ralph Guldahl won the Open at Oakland Hills. Sam finished second and won $800. But he also won $500 for being the best-dressed player—which meant that he left the course with $300 more than the champion.

Arnold Palmer played a practice round with Paul Goydos at the 1996 Masters. Goydos had won Palmer's Bay Hill tournament just a few weeks before, and following their round Palmer invited Goydos to join him for a beer in the champions' locker room.

Now, Goydos is a fine player, but he is a little on the heavy side, at 5'9" and 200 or so pounds.

"Sam, this is Paul Goydos," said Palmer. He won my tournament at Bay Hill."

"You did?" Sam asked.

Sam Snead and Ted Williams met at the height of their respective careers and became good friends. They shared the same agent—Fred Corcoran—as well as a love of hunting and fishing.

One day Sam was sitting in the Red Sox dugout prior to a game against the Yankees. The subject turned to hitting.

"Ted said that he tried to hit the ball hard with his top [left] hand," Sam remembered. "He felt that gave him the most power and control. I said that I liked to lead into the hitting area with my left hand in control and then pour it on at the last second with my right hand. Well, Ted being Ted, we got into a big discussion about it. He disagreed, but I could tell he was thinking hard about what I said. Sure enough, he went 0-for-4 that afternoon. You should have heard some of the things he called me after the game."

Most people know that Sam never won a U.S. Open, but for all his impressive wins around the world, there was one other tournament Sam Snead had never won—a club championship. That's not surprising, since he turned pro virtually right out of high school.

All that changed when the board of directors at Pine Tree voted to let Sam play in their club championship. Still, there was no guarantee Sam would win in a walk. Not with a membership that included the likes of amateur greats Dale Morey, Ed Tutwiler, and Bill Hyndman. Even so, it shouldn't surprise anyone that Sam won. Easily.

When Sam turned eighty, the Homestead decided to honor him with a golf tournament and dinner. At the dinner, officials from Bath County, Virginia (one stoplight for the entire county), unveiled a large road sign that showed an image of Sam and announced that this was his birthplace.

Sam studied the sign for a moment.

"You know, folks," he said, "this looks real nice right now, but just wait until hunting season, when it becomes a target for those old boys up in the hills."

After a few years on the Tour, Sam became friendly with Jimmy Demaret and arranged for him to come to the Homestead for an exhibition. When Demaret arrived, he looked around the tiny town of Hot Springs and asked Sam what they could do for some excitement. Sam thought for a few seconds, then said, "Well, Jimmy, it's Saturday night. We could go down to the barbershop and watch a few of the boys get haircuts."

Many years ago, Sam played an exhibition match at a course in Virginia against Jay Randolph. This was sort of a big deal in Virginia, since Jay was a popular announcer for NBC Sports and the son of a longtime, powerful U.S. senator from Virginia, Jennings Randolph. More important, from

Sam's point of view, was the fact that Jay was a good player—his competitive career capped by winning the Egyptian Open.

It wasn't likely that Sam was going to lose, but just to be on the safe side, he wasn't taking any chances.

"Junior, no newspaper scores today," he said to Jay on the first tee. "We're playing everything out."

To nobody's surprise—least of all Randolph's—Sam won. Handily.

One day a friend stopped by Sam's house in Florida for a visit. As he made his way up the front walk he noticed an odd-looking contraption set off in the flowers. It was a wooden box with one side held up by elastic bands.

"What's that thing, Sam?" the friend asked.

"It's a rabbit trap I made," Sam said proudly. "Those rabbits have been coming around here and eating all my flowers. It's costing me a fortune."

The friend cast a skeptical eye at the trap, which looked for all the world like the product of a junior high shop class.

"This thing works?" the friend asked.

"Hell yes, it works," Sam said. "I caught one the other day. It's in the freezer all skinned out. I'm giving it to the maid."

Sure enough, there was a rabbit in the freezer, ready for cooking.

Sam has a remarkable affection for—and understanding of—wildlife. One morning, during the 1988 U.S. Amateur at the nearby Homestead, Sam was walking around his farm with a writer friend. When they came to a pond, Sam stuck his forefinger in the water and splashed it around. A large bass swam over and gently closed its mouth over Sam's finger. Sam ran his left hand along the length of the fish, and then slowly pulled his hand out of the water, with the bass still attached to his finger. He talked to the fish for a moment, then slid it back gently into the pond.

Sam has a phenomenal memory for tournaments he has played in over the years. One day a fan came up to him and said how much he enjoyed watching Sam play.

"I saw you once in New Orleans," the man said. "You played the greatest shot I've ever seen."

"It was on the 15th hole," Sam said.

"That's right," the man replied.

"I drove the ball down onto the side of a ditch," Sam said.

"That's right," the man said.

"I took a 3-wood and carved the prettiest little shot off that bank to about three feet from the hole," Sam said.

"My God, you're right, Sam!" exclaimed the man.

"And I missed the damned putt," Sam said, laughing.

While Sam would seek out his brothers—Homer, Jess, and Pete—for help when his swing wasn't quite right, the truth is that like most players of his generation, he was largely self-taught. It helped that he was a great natural athlete and had a keen eye for adapting what he saw in other sports to the game of golf.

One afternoon, when he was in his seventies, Sam was watching a baseball game on television when a player hit a towering home run. The player's swing was replayed in slow motion and the announcer mentioned the man's outstanding arm extension that generated so much power.

"As soon as he said it, a light went off in my head," Sam recalled. "I realized that as I had gotten older I had gotten a little lazy and hadn't been extending my arms when I hit the ball."

The next time Sam went out to play, that was the only swing key that he focused upon. He was playing the Lower Cascades course with some friends, and to say that the key worked is an understatement. He tied the course record—a feat made all the sweeter because the record had been held by Sam's nephew, J. C. Snead.

"I've always been flattered when people ask for my autograph, but I can't even imagine what it must be like for Sam," Dave Marr once said as he watched Sam work his way through a crowd of fans. "He's been signing autographs for sixty years. That's an awful lot of autographs."

And interrupted dinners.

One night Sam was having dinner with a writer friend when a woman approached and asked for his autograph. Sam was very polite, asking her if she played golf, where she was from, and so on. When he handed her the autograph, she thanked him. She should have quit while she was ahead.

"We've always loved watching you, Mr. [Gay] Brewer," she said, as she returned to her table.

What made this all the more incredible was that it took place in Sam Snead's Tavern, in his hometown, Hot Springs, Virginia.

Sam was hugely popular throughout the South, but nowhere did he have more fans than in Greensboro, North Carolina, where he won the tournament eight times between 1938 and 1965. His galleries were always huge and partisan— as Lloyd Mangrum found out one year when he and Sam dueled in the final round. If Sam's ball was headed over a green or into the woods, it would miraculously bounce off one of his fans. Finally, after seeing Sam get yet another good break, it got to be too much for Mangrum.

"How can I win?" he asked. "I'm playing Sam, God, and all these people."

A writer once asked Sam if he always shot at the pin or whether he liked to be safe and play to the fat part of the green. Sam looked at the man as if he were crazy.

"Well, I shoot at the pins," he said.

"Why?" the writer asked.

"'Cause that's what they're there for," Sam replied.

For proof, he could have cited his record for holes-in-one. He's made thirty-five in all—and he's made them with every club in the bag, from a driver and a 1-iron through a pitching wedge.

LEFTY STACKHOUSE

Lefty Stackhouse was a talented golfer, but he's probably best known for a fairly volcanic temper. Now, there are times when getting mad can help you play better, but that was seldom the case with Lefty.

Playing in the final round of a tournament that he had a chance to win, he hit a wild hook off the tee on a par 3 and watched as it sailed out of bounds. He slammed down his club and raked his right hand through a nearby rosebush, cutting it badly.

Still, that wasn't enough. He glared at his left hand—which equally offended him—and growled, "You're next."

CURTIS STRANGE

A writer once asked Curtis Strange what he thought was the greatest strength in his game. Strange thought for a moment and then said, "I've never fooled myself—either as a player or a person."

So, at the lowest point in his career, he was brutally honest. It came on the last day of the 1995 Ryder Cup matches. He had been one of Lanny Wadkins's two captain's picks—and many people had been critical of Wadkins's decision.

In the final day's singles matches, Strange had drawn England's Nick Faldo, whom he beat in a playoff at the 1988 U.S. Open at The Country Club. The match was close throughout, but in the end Strange—who always prided himself on his ability to hit the big shot under pressure—lost. He was devastated.

"No matter how hard the press rips me, they won't be nearly as hard on me as I'll be on myself," he said.

TEMPER, TEMPER

Like many good players, 1996 Canadian Open champion Dudley Hart had a fairly healthy temper as a kid. He also had a father who was a golf professional and mightily disapproved of his son's outbursts—especially when they resulted in broken clubs.

Young Dudley thought he'd discovered a way to keep all this from his father. When Dad was out of the shop, Dudley would reshaft his broken clubs. And like teenagers everywhere, he was sure he had pulled one over on Dear Old Dad.

Wrong.

"I knew I was in trouble when he finally pointed out to me that he'd never seen a set of clubs that were so mismatched," Dudley admitted. "Every shaft in the set was different."

Ky Laffoon was one of the best—and most colorful—players on the Tour during the 1930s. But for all his skills, his play was often overshadowed by his temper, which he took no pains to repress.

"The Chief," as he was known, got into an argument with Johnny Bulla in a locker room following their round. It's important to note that there wasn't much backdown in Bulla, either, and pretty soon they were going at it full bore—until Laffoon picked Bulla up and threw him on top of a row of lockers and refused to let him down until cooler heads prevailed and got Laffoon out the door.

It used to be said that Fred Corcoran, the Boston Irishman who served as the PGA's tournament director in the early days of the Tour and also got the LPGA off the ground, didn't have an enemy in the world. But on at least one occasion, he ran head-on into a guy who, if not an enemy, wasn't exactly a friend.

Corcoran was holding court—which he did better than anyone in the game's history—in the old Del Monte Lodge just off the 18th green at Pebble Beach during the Crosby. Dick Metz, a pro from Texas, walked in and accused Corcoran of favoring the touring professionals at the expense of the teaching pros in the field. Corcoran offered to buy Metz a drink and tried to calm him down. But Corcoran's considerable charms were lost on Metz, who knocked Corcoran out with a solid right to the jaw.

DICK TETTELBACH

The late Dick Tettelbach served for several years as the president of the Connecticut State Golf Association, but he was best known in the state as a former captain of the Yale baseball team—and teammate of President George Bush.

Tettelbach was good enough to spend a few years in the major leagues, first with the Yankees and then with the Washington Senators. But he always kept his baseball accomplishments in perspective—witness this story he happily told about one of his career highlights.

In his first game with the Senators, he hit a home run. He rounded the bases and returned to the dugout, marveling at the huge roar from the stands.

"I don't want to hurt your feelings, but they're not cheering for you, kid," growled a veteran player. "Ike just entered the park."

LEE TREVINO

Like any great player, Lee Trevino has a healthy ego. But when the time came for him to play in his final British Open, the two-time champion did so quietly. The year was 1995 and the Open was being played at St. Andrews. Trevino knew it would be his final British Open, but he told just a few close friends. Why?

Because this was also Arnold Palmer's final British Open, and Trevino didn't want to do anything that would shift the spotlight—even if ever so slightly—from the man Trevino knew had done so much to build the popularity of the championship. And the game.

Lee Trevino grew up in Dallas and learned to play on municipal courses that weren't always in the best shape. One time he was playing in a tournament where some of the pros were complaining about the sorry condition of the course. Not Trevino, though.

"For the money they're paying us, I'd be happy to play in a dried-up riverbed," he told the writers. "Of course, I can play a dried-up riverbed better than any of these guys."

HARRY VARDON

England's Harry Vardon won—among other things—a record six British Opens and the 1900 U.S. Open. Following his U.S. Open win he embarked on a long and profitable exhibition tour of America. When he arrived in Aiken, South Carolina, he was joined by the Prince of Wales for a round at the Palmetto Golf Club. The members were thrilled to have His Royal Highness as a guest, but less impressed by the best golfer in the world.

They refused to let him into the clubhouse.

They refused to let him wear knickers on the course—a privilege restricted to "gentlemen."

And he had to get a special dispensation from the club's golf committee allowing him to smoke on the course.

KEN VENTURI

K en Venturi was very close to his father, and their relationship did much to fuel his drive to become one of the
game's great champions.

"My father understood people and what makes them tick,"
Venturi remembers. "When I won the San Francisco City
Championship—which was really a big deal in those days—
he said to me, 'So what? Do you have any idea how many
cities there are in this country?' When I won the California
Amateur, he said, 'That's nice, but there are forty-seven other
states that have championships.' Even after I won the U.S.
Open, he wasn't that impressed. He told me that it wouldn't
count for that much unless I backed it up with another win—
which, fortunately, I did.

"But after I won the 1966 Lucky International in San
Francisco, I began to have problems with my hands. I went
to the Mayo Clinic, and the doctor was very honest with me.
He told me that gangrene had set in and it was very serious.
He told me to go back home to San Francisco and get my
affairs in order. He said that there was a very good chance
that some of my fingers might have to be amputated.

"When the time came for me to leave San Francisco and
go have the surgery, my father drove me to the airport," Venturi continues. "I told him what the doctor had said. He was

quiet, then he hugged me and said, 'Ken, it doesn't matter if you never hit another golf ball. You were the best I ever saw.'"

When Ken Venturi turned pro in 1956, the PGA Tour was a much different place than it is today. Purses were much smaller and, as a result, it wasn't all that unusual for players to resort to gamesmanship—especially when they were paired with a young player.

"Some of the older players would try and test you," Venturi explained once. "One player in particular would stand very close to the tee and just as you started your swing he'd begin to walk. The movement was just enough to catch your eye and disrupt your concentration. I got tired of it, and the next time we reached a tee I decided to do something about it. I set up over the ball and started my swing. Sure enough, the guy started to walk and I froze at the top of my swing.

"'Do that again and the next thing I hit with this driver is going to be you,' I said.

"He never bothered me again."

LANNY WADKINS

At the heart of it, golf is a very individual game. While it's possible to share the credit for a victory, the blame for defeat rests squarely on a player's shoulders alone. Maybe that's why team events like the Walker Cup, Curtis Cup, and Ryder Cup bring out remarkable sportsmanship in the people who play in them. There's no better example than the sacrifice Lanny Wadkins made in the 1993 Ryder Cup at the Belfry in England.

Wadkins is the supreme competitor, a player of such confidence that it's said he can swagger from a sitting position. He is especially fierce in match play, so it's easy to imagine how excited he was on the eve of the final day's singles play in the '93 Ryder Cup.

But before the team captains could set their lineups for the singles matches, there came word that Scotland's Sam Torrance might have to sit out because of a foot injury. This put the American captain, Tom Watson, in a difficult position: it required him to put a player's name "in the envelope." In the event Torrance couldn't play, that American player would have to sit out the last day's play. Watson anguished over the decision. The score was close, and pulling the wrong player could cost his team the Cup. More tellingly, putting a player in the envelope implied he was the weakest player on the squad.

Knowing how difficult Watson's decision was, Wadkins—who joined the Tour in the same year as Watson—volunteered to go in the envelope.

At the American team breakfast prior to the Sunday matches, an emotional Watson spoke to his team.

"Every match we play today will have a little bit of Lanny in it," he said. "If your match is getting a little too tough, think about Lanny."

The Americans went on to win, and to a man, his teammates gave a lot of the credit to Lanny Wadkins.

CYRIL WALKER

England's Cyril Walker was thirty when he won the 1924 U.S. Open at Oakland Hills, beating Bobby Jones by three strokes. He was so thrilled by his victory that he paid his caddie the astonishing sum of $500—the amount of the winner's purse.

Several months after winning the Open, Walker arrived on the first tee at the Los Angeles Open.

"Mr. Walker, are you the winner of any state opens?" the starter asked him.

"All goddamn forty-eight at once," he replied sharply.

Despite his win at the Open, Walker wound up as some-thing of a sad—even tragic—figure.

Whatever money he earned as a player was lost in a failed real estate venture in Florida. In 1937, fourteen years after his greatest victory, the U.S. Open returned to Oakland Hills. The club invited Walker back to honor his victory, and put him up in one of the area's best hotels. When the tournament ended, Walker refused to leave the hotel. His last years were spent as a caddie—a fine pastime for someone who loves the game, but not for an Open champion.

TOM WATSON

Tom Watson was in Scotland for the 1992 British Open at Muirfield. That year one of the courses used for qualifying was North Berwick. All day long, Tom Watson had watched from his hotel room as players tried to cope with the unique and difficult 16th green. The elevated green is bisected by a four-foot-deep gully. A shot hit to the wrong side of the gully leaves a player with an extremely difficult putt.

As Watson watched, he became more and more intrigued by the green and the problems it presented. After the close of play, Watson left the hotel in the gathering darkness and went to try a few shots to the green.

At the same time, the club's groundskeeper, Stewart Greenwood, was leaving the course to return home after a long and tiring day. He looked over and saw a solitary figure out by the 16th green. Greenwood made his way to the green and sternly told the man that the course was closed to play and asked him if he would please leave.

The five-time British Open champion—his curiosity satisfied—did.

TOM WEISKOPF

Throughout his career, Tom Weiskopf has been compared—perhaps unfairly—to Jack Nicklaus. They both grew up in Ohio and played golf for Ohio State. There's no question Weiskopf was a better player for his years competing against Nicklaus, but sometimes the similarities got to be too much—like at the 1978 Masters.

Both players arrived on the first tee for the final round in identical blue slacks and striped shirts. That was it for Weiskopf, who sent for another shirt and changed on the tee.

THE WILD KINGDOM

Golf coexists with nature. That is how it should be. It's just that some times the two coexist better than other times. Take, for example, the scandalous death of a Canada goose (*Branta canadensis*) that was killed at Congressional Country Club in 1979.

Reports of the goose's untimely demise differed. Naturally.

Defenders of Dr. Sherman A. Thomas, the man charged in the slaying, claim that the doctor hit the bird with his approach shot and, seeing that it was dying, simply put it out of its misery with a couple whacks of his putter—model unknown, but a mallet seems more appropriate.

Dr. Thomas's accusers, however, charged that the bird honked while the doctor was putting, causing him to miss and so enraging him that he chased down the offending animal and clubbed it to death.

It should come as no surprise that there is a federal law that prohibits this sort of thing. Apparently something called the Migratory Bird Treaty Act proscribes the means by which a Canada goose may be dispatched. A golf club to the head does not qualify.

Nor should anyone be surprised that (a) the case became a cause célèbre in Washington among environmentalists, people who loathe golf, and the usual common scolds; and

(b) the defense requested a jury trial (your tax dollars and legal system at work).

In the end, the doctor cut a deal with prosecutors, agreeing to plead guilty to "Hunting out of season" and paying a $500 fine.

The corpse, by the way, is still missing.

TIGER WOODS

Tiger Woods's father, Earl, is only a casual golfer, but he understands that at the highest levels golf is as much a mental game as it is a physical challenge. As a former Green Beret who served in Vietnam, he knows something about mental toughness—and how to instill it in another person.

"When Tiger was growing up I would pressure him until he almost reached his breaking point, but I was very careful never to go too far," he once explained. "I told Tiger, 'I promise you, you'll never meet another person as naturally tough as you.' And he hasn't. And he won't."

Whatever he did, he must have done something right. He must have done a lot of somethings right.

INDEX

Snead, Sam, 10–11,
51, 55,
78, 99, 146, 154–55,
159, 160,
168–77
Spanish PGA
Championship,
18
Spiller, Bill, 166
Sproul, John 77
St. Andrews
Cathedral, 105
St. Andrews Gold
Club, 150
Stackhouse, Lefty,
178
Stokes, Pappy, 26
Stranahan, Frank,
166
Stepp, Howie, 151
Strange, Curtis,
179
Suggs, Louise, 19
Sullivan, Ed, 10
Sutton, Hal, 34

T
Taft, President
William
Howard, 141
Taylor, Dick, 118,
143
Temper, 180–81
"Temporary Rules,
1941"
(Richmond Golf
Club, London),
106

Tettelbach, Dick,
182
Texas Rangers, 102
Thomas, Dr.
Sherman A.,
197–98
Thomson, Mary
(Mrs. Peter),
49–51
Thomson, Peter, 49,
68
Tillinghast, A. W.,
6
Timms, Cecil, 28
Torrance, Sam, 190
Toski, Bob, 71
Townsend, Ron, 16
Tracy, Spencer,
164–65
Trent Jones, Robert,
2, 3, 4, 5,
14, 74, 91, 160–61
Trevino, Lee, 169,
183–85
Tutwiler, Ed, 171
Tyre Jones, Robert,
4

V
Vardon, Harry, 125,
143, 186
Vare, Glenna Collett,
19–20
Venturi, Ken, 29, 64,
77, 78, 166,
187–89
Vicenzo, Roberto de,
74–75

W
Wadkins, Lanny,
65–66, 179,
190–91
Walker, Cyril, 192
Warner Brothers, 89
Watson, Dennis,
156
Watson, Tom, 111,
190, 194–95
Weiskopf, Jeanne
(Mrs. Tom), 59
Weiskopf, Tom, 59,
117, 119, 129,
196
Whitaker, Jack, 101
Whittmore, Burt,
155–56
Williams, Ted,
170–71
Wind, Herbert
Warren, 93,
94–95
Winged Foot, 6
Woods, Earl, 199
Woods, Tiger, 48, 57,
119, 159, 166,
199
Wood, Willie, 34
World War II, 40,
106–108

Y
Yancey, Bert, 59

Z
Zaharias, Babe, 19
Zoeller, Fuzzy, 101